J. Harold T

Oct. 12

(READ ON TRAIN GOING TO HARRIS-
BURG, PA. OCT. 12ᵗʰ for THE FUNERAL
of "POPPY."— DR. C. WALDO CHERRY—
OCT. 13. 1944.)

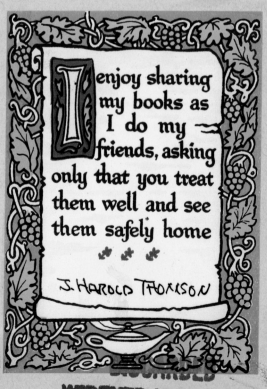

CAN WE STILL BELIEVE IN IMMORTALITY?

FREDERICK C. GRANT

Professor of Biblical Theology
Union Theological Seminary
New York City

Can We Still Believe In Immortality?

THE CLOISTER PRESS ✦ Louisville
MCMXLIV

Books in Wartime

The order of the War Production Board limiting the
paper to be used for books makes it necessary to reduce
the thickness of the paper used. As a result the books
look thinner—in some instances by almost a half—than
they would under normal conditions. But this is done
to conserve vital materials for the war needs.

TO THE MEMORY OF

My Mother

WHOSE WHOLE LIFE
BORE THE TESTIMONY
THAT GOODNESS IS
SUPREME AND EVERLASTING

Beloved, now are we the children of God, and it is not yet made manifest what we shall be. We know that, if he shall be manifested, we shall be like him; for we shall see him even as he is. And every one that hath this hope set on him purifieth himself, even as he is pure.

—I John iii. 2-3.

Things which eye saw not, and ear heard not,
And which entered not into the heart of man,
Whatsoever things God prepared for them that love him.

—I Corinthians ii. 9.

O God, who hast prepared for those who love thee such good things as pass man's understanding; Pour into our hearts such love toward thee, that we, loving thee above all things, may obtain thy promises, which exceed all that we can desire; through Jesus Christ our Lord. *Amen.*

—Collect for the Sixth Sunday after Trinity.

Foreword

SURVIVAL after death is the most persistent of man's beliefs regarding himself and the universe in which he lives. The origins of this confidence antedate history. The belief has drawn strength from almost every historical religion, in one form or another, and has in turn supported their claims to spiritual and moral authority. In ages when materialism or superstition was dominant, it has persisted in spite of this deterrent influence, as a conviction deeper than reason, a longing as unquenchable as life itself. Indeed, the depth and vitality of its roots in history and in human nature are indicated by the fact that men have insisted upon believing it in the face of threatened terrors in the great beyond, worse than death itself, from which extinction in the grave might conceivably have been a welcome refuge. And although forty centuries of thought and speculation, of ardent yearning and experiment, have not thus far succeeded in making it a truth "evident unto all men," nevertheless, the trustworthiness of the belief has been assumed by much of the noblest ethics and by many of the noblest characters in history. Immortality may not be finally and indisputably proved, but it may at least be claimed that belief in it makes possible a higher kind of life, a kind of life all but universally recognized as higher, than the assumption that man's life ends forever at death. Immortality may not be scientifically demonstrated, but its truth has to be assumed in order to make fully reasonable the higher life of man.

It is this persistent, deeply rooted, characteristically human hope that men still instinctively hold in our day, often in the face of assumed contradictions of science. For many people now believe that modern science and philosophy have rendered the belief, at least in its traditional Christian form, untenable. A conflict is set up between "heart" and "head" which only the arbitrary "will to believe" can end: a solution which many persons find themselves unable to accept. It is the purpose of this book to examine the traditional form of belief in life after death, to distinguish between what is essential and what is transitory in the formulation of the doctrine, and to inquire whether or not or in how far a true reading of modern science and philosophy makes necessary either the abandonment or modification of the belief.

The field is wide, as wide as the thought and interests of the modern world. One cannot hope to deal with the subject exhaustively, but only to consider some of its salient problems. Indeed, modern thought, even in the scientific field, is far from final at the present time. In every generation, "modern" thought means contemporary thought; and since the intellectual outlook of men is ever in constant process of change, no "modern" thought is ever final. By the time finality is achieved, that thought has already entered the past. Only the past, therefore, can give us a fully rounded and comprehensive set of ideas. Instead of a finally formulated system like that of the thirteenth century, "modern thought" represents a vast tendency, a slow, solar progression whose limits no man has set and whose precise bearings upon Christian doctrine cannot yet be stated. The subterranean hell has vanished; the literal seven heavens of Jewish and early Christian eschatology are recognized as imaginary; but the exacter relations of science and faith are still far from definitely determined. And it remains an open question if science, in the end, instead of requiring the abandonment of faith in immortality may not demand its restoration. Only so, perhaps, will the mysterious phenomenon of *life* in this otherwise dull, decadent corner of the material universe be made intelligible, and the cosmos be viewed once more as the fit tabernacle of a divine, all-wise Spirit, in whose eternal existence the soul of man has share. Moreover, it is only as men come to lay hold upon a life *worth* making immortal, and become conscious of ends or purposes whose realization carries on beyond the confines of this world of time, space, and matter, that faith in a life to come will begin once more to seem reasonable and necessary.

The plan of this book is first to consider the origin of the Christian belief in eternal life, its sources and development in the early days of Christian history, and its formulation in the Church's traditional teaching, both Catholic and Protestant; then to examine the status of the belief in modern thought and the influences which have affected men's views; finally, to consider the question, "Can we still believe in immortality —specifically, in immortality as described by traditional, orthodox Christianity?"

Emerson wrote in his *Journal*, "I notice that as soon as writers broach this question they begin to quote. I hate quotations. Tell me what you know" (May, 1849). But if ever quotation is excusable it is surely in dealing with the testimony of men's deepest convictions regarding life after death. What we are doing is, in effect, to ask them to tell us "what they know." Moreover, it is difficult to see how a survey of "modern thought" can dispense with citation of the words of modern authors. Better the exact utterance of the witnesses themselves than the paraphrase of some self-appointed interpreter, especially in gathering the testimony of scientists and philosophers whose own words convey the freshness and vividness of personal conviction. Indeed, despite his injunction, one cannot forego quoting Emerson's own later words, from the *Journal:* "The blazing evidence of immortality is our dissatisfaction with any other solution" (July, 1855). What could state more clearly or vividly Emerson's conviction than these words? I will not apologize, then, for my quotations. And if it turns out that these are the best part of my book, or even its only claim to merit, I shall, like a good lawyer, be content to rest my case, not upon my own brief, but upon the evidence adduced by the witnesses.

On account of the paper shortage all footnotes have been omitted, though the Bibliography has been retained. The Table of Contents will have to serve in lieu of an index.

Contents

PAGE

WHY THE QUESTION IS ASKED 1

The modern problem: Must we abandon belief in
immortality? Can religion dispense with it? Or ethics? Psychical Research and Spiritualism. The situation crucial for Christianity, which cannot dispense
with the belief.

I. THE CHRISTIAN BELIEF IN IMMORTALITY 11

Advantages of philosophy and "natural religion" enjoyed by early Christianity. Rise of the doctrine of
immortality in pre-Christian Judaism. Influence of
other religions. Martyrdom of the faithful in the
days of the Maccabees. The expression of the doctrine in apocalyptic literature. Resurrection and the
future life.

The teaching of Jesus. His reticence combined
with positiveness. Christ as represented in the
Fourth Gospel. Traces of a more materialistic conception in the gospels. Christ's human temperament. The fact of Jesus' resurrection. Historical
evidence and the sense of congruity. The earliest
apostolic preaching based upon experience. The
resurrection narratives in the New Testament.

St. Paul's rationale of the resurrection. The early
Christian inheritance from Judaism. Eschatology
and mysticism. The later New Testament literature.
The *Apocalypse of John*. The Johannine Epistles.

Literature of the second and third centuries. Interpretation of Scripture. Christianity *vs*. paganism.
A new force in Mediterranean religion. The Apolo-

PAGE

gists. The inheritance of Hellenistic religion, philosophy, and science. *Resurrectio carnis.* "Deification." The Christian Platonists. The Patristic formulation of Christian eschatology.

Catholic "comprehension." Purgatory. Mediaeval and Reformation theology. The modern shifting of interest. Protestant and Catholic emphases and interpretations. Summary of the traditional Christian doctrine. Dante. The *Theologia Germanica.*

II. IMMORTALITY IN MODERN THOUGHT 67

Declining influence of the doctrine. Vagueness of present-day beliefs. Effect of modern science. The war. Current tendencies. "Nature's latest experiment." Man's homelessness in the universe. Astronomy and geology. The doctrine of evolution. Defect of imagination. The "objective" world of science.

Modern biology and psychology. The phenomena of life and intelligence. Energy. Life essentially immaterial. The biological significance of death. Man "organic to nature." Relations between mind and brain. The "secretion" theory of mind now discarded. The primacy of mind. Survival neither impossible nor improbable. Consonance with the Christian conception. Problem of *origin* of the soul or self. Immortality in palaeolithic times. Immortality of lower animals. Survival of memory. Statistics of belief. The Psychical Research questionnaire. Universality of law and order. Has science the last word on the subject? The spiritualizing of science. The rights of man in a physical universe. The future of the cosmos. Degradation of energy. The spiritual interpretation of nature.

Philosophy and the problem of survival. Its scientific character. Emphasis upon imponderable val-

ues. The trend toward symbolism and mysticism.
"Nothing that really is can cease to be." Personality.
Is it destined to be absorbed in the Absolute? Even
so, it survives. Comparison with Hinduism. Human personality conceived as already existing in the
Absolute. The "eternal now." "Absorption" understood by the analogy of love. The problem of time.
Origin of the conception of eternity in religious experience. Mystic union in the cults of Orpheus and
Dionysus. Translation to another mode of existence
vs. mere continuity in endless time. Time our measure of the slowing-down of energy. Time coeval
with creation. Symbolic value of the time-concept.
Time embraced "within" eternity. Initiation into
ultimate reality.

The "Moral Argument" in its modern form. Is
immortality desirable? A noble life the strongest
argument for immortality. "Death does not count"
in certain states. Eudaemonism and future rewards.
Compensation of individuals not an unjust demand.
Immortality and modern social thought. The instinct for life and the hunger for fellowship cannot
remain forever frustrate. A foretaste and pledge of
future fulfillment.

III. CAN WE STILL BELIEVE IN IMMORTALITY? .. 120

"Proofs" of immortality lacking. Still an object of
faith. Probability vs. demonstrations. The modern
world-view does not disprove belief, but requires another formulation. Science requires us to think in
terms of a transcendent self-realization impossible in
this world. The disappearance of "empirical evidences" not altogether a loss. Christ and Spinoza.
Lack of concrete imagery. The self not identical
with the physical body. Socrates' words to his disciples.

PAGE

Science renders difficult the form in which hope formerly was expressed, not the hope itself. The goal of Ultimate Good found in Christ. Spiritual experience, not logical proof, underlies Christian conviction. Value of Christ's resurrection for faith in Him, to which faith in immortality is secondary. Christian immortality centered in union with Christ. It thus lies upon a plane beyond the reach of science or of history. Must the traditional formulation be radically modified? Probation in this life. Theology and ethics both involved. Tremendous issues of this present life. The optimism of "natural immortality" not infallible. *Faith* in immortality, if not immortality itself, morally conditioned.

Specific doctrines: The Intermediate State and its corollaries. Prayers for the departed. Invocation of saints. Spiritual progress really endless. The joy of heaven. A progressive transformation. Experience of prayer in war-time. Reality the only true test. Heaven and Hell in primitive religion, in Jewish eschatology, and in religious psychology. The appeal of universalism to the modern mind. Eternal Justice. Hell the penalty of spurning love. Need for a truer symbol of retribution. The Resurrection of the Body. Persistence and Identity. The Last Judgment. Right forever right and Wrong always wrong. The Immediate Judgment. The Consummation and Eternal Bliss. Personal immortality. Love the guiding power of the universe and "the hierophant of all the divine mysteries." Personality made perfect in unselfish love.

A SELECTED BIBLIOGRAPHY 150

Why the Question is Asked

"If in this life we have nothing more than a hope, in Christ, we are of all men most to be pitied." It is apparently the destiny of many in our generation to put these words to the test, and to discover whatever residuum of Christian faith remains when belief in immortality has grown weak and dim. The strong, "sufficient grounds" which stayed our fathers' faith have ceased to satisfy many persons at the present day. Not only do the "evidences" once adduced fail to carry conviction, but our whole outlook upon life has so completely shifted that this failure is often felt to be no great loss. Many, including some who would be Christians, feel little or no reluctance in abandoning the belief. The whole question is shelved; it has simply ceased to be significant. "One world at a time," they would doubtless reply with Thoreau, if pressed for an explanation. The demands of this life, the widely recognized responsibility for corporate and social tasks, the various manifold interests of the day have swept into the steady foreground of men's consciousness: there is no need for recourse to "supernaturalism" or to motives of fear or hope for the future in order to ensure correct social action. If personality survives, well and good; but if not, let us make the most of this life!

Hath man no second life? *Pitch this one high!*

1

There have been ages in the past when immortality was a closed question. Men no more doubted survival after death than they doubted the flatness of the earth or tomorrow's sunrise in the east. It was an essential part of the common religious tradition, and without it religion was inconceivable. Hence it was not so much proved as taken for granted. Its value was axiomatic. But today all this is changed. Not only has a large part of the superstructure of religious tradition been swept away, but many are debating whether or not the ancient substructure is worth preserving. Why not make a clean sweep and begin again, founding religious faith and practice upon the more readily demonstrable and immediately appreciable motives of social idealism? Let us do away with the impractical otherworldliness of mediaeval and conventional Christianity, and found a system nearer to the heart's desire—a desire, many will say, for something profoundly *more* than endlessness of individual life.

Few persons can be found today who share the sentiment of Tennyson, "If immortality be not true, then no God but a mocking fiend created us. . . . I'd sink my head tonight in a chloroformed handkerchief and have done with it all!" The argument seems strangely unreal and the sentiment artificial. Its tenor is that of a line or two in the Lesson in the traditional Burial Office: "What advantageth it me, if the dead rise not? Let us eat and drink, for tomorrow we die"—words whose cruel logic so painfully shocked Huxley in an hour of personal bereavement. But we sense at once, today, the fallacy of this argument (for which, perhaps, the English version—or the underlying quotation—is more responsible than St. Paul): "If the dead rise not, let us turn hedonists and epicureans, and give up all effort toward higher ends than mere pleasure." A false, unreal minor-premise is here assumed, which few are willing to admit: "The only good in life is the satisfaction of personal needs or demands; therefore make the best of it, or endure the worst of it, and prepare for heaven; nothing short of a life to come can recompense us for the painful virtues which must be exercised in this one." The fallacy is patent; and there are those who conclude that any and every belief in immortality is accordingly either the result of rationalizing, the fruit of a will to believe in which the wish is father to the thought; or else it is some form of hoax devised in the long ago "to keep the masses in subjection," offering them sugar-plums in another world in lieu of justice here, a fictitious sanction to enforce and guarantee a priest-made code of morals and religion.

However, not all persons who abandon faith in immortality share this view. There are "those of the nobler sort" who scorn reward for doing well; for whom the threat of everlasting punishment is meaningless; who view tenderly and sympathetically the hope which has stirred in the breasts of countless human generations; but who simply do not know, and "will not venture beyond the evidence." For them it is no longer "morally necessary" to assume immortality or the existence of God as its guarantor—as did Sir William Hamilton, who held that "a God is . . . only of practical interest, inasmuch as He is the condition of our immortality." For them, as for Spinoza, happiness is not the reward of virtue, for virtue itself is happiness. And it never occurs to them to inquire, when confronted by a compelling moral imperative, "What is there in it for me?" Their first concern is for the future of their ideals, the survival of the true, the beautiful, and good, the things lovely and of good report in whose service their daily lives are freely spent. Theirs is the spirit of the soldier who asks, returning to consciousness in the dressing-station, "Did we take the objective?" and has no thought for himself. They readily admit that they do not expect to see the complete triumph of these ideals in their own lifetime, or even the full fruition of other and lesser aims inspired by these far visions of perfection. They feel that whatever the future holds, they are here and now sharers in a wider life which is completely worth while from moment to moment. With the disciples on the mount they confess, "It is good for us to be here." Not for their own private destinies are they concerned but for something far more important, they will say; namely, the high aims and goals of their ceaseless striving. That *these* should fail or be blotted

out, as Pringle-Pattison has said, "that our ideals themselves should perish, that nothing worth existing should
have any pledge of continuance or growth, that the
world of values, in short, should have no relation to the
world of facts—that is the one intolerable conclusion.
And just because its intolerableness has nothing to do
with any private hopes or fears, we feel that the refusal
to entertain it is a judgment of objective validity, that
it is, in short, of the same texture as the inability to
believe an intellectual contradiction."

§

This high, heroic attitude cannot, however, be said
to be universal in our day. Not many will be found
willing to abandon the hope of personal survival if
only their ideals live on. Nor will many see the necessity of a choice between the two, or the significance of
"values" if the persons to whom they were "valuable"
cease to exist. It is much more probable that the great
majority of those who are unable to profess belief in
immortality feel a genuine reluctance at parting with
the age-long hope. The eagerness with which the investigations of the Society for Psychical Research have
been followed, as well as other and similar experiments,
proves men's readiness to be convinced. Popular interest in Spiritualism, especially since World War I,
affords similar proof. And for many others the formulation of their own negative convictions comes with a

shock—the discovery, resulting either from scientific study of Nature or as inference from the data of their own experience, that

> the world, which seems
> To lie before us like a land of dreams,
> So various, so beautiful, so new,
> Hath really neither joy, nor love, nor light,
> Nor certitude, nor peace, nor help for pain.

A note of sadness inevitably steals into our thoughts as we reflect upon the gradual loss of this faith in the course of our own lives, or in those of men in general during recent generations. Even granting its baseless-ness in fact, as some persons find they must, the belief certainly lent a value to this present life which nothing else has supplied or can supply. As a friend of mine once confessed, "I almost wish I had been born in an-other age, when belief was easier, and that I had not lived to see the decline of faith in our day." This feel-ing was Arnold's in *Dover Beach:*

> The sea of faith
> Was once, too, at the full, and round earth's shore
> Lay like the folds of a bright girdle furled.
> But now I only hear
> Its melancholy, long, withdrawing roar,
> Retreating, to the breath
> Of the night-wind, down the vast edges drear
> And naked shingles of the world.

"If in this life we have nothing more than a hope"; if even the figure of Christ represents only heroic abandonment, the supreme wager with death in all the history of our race, but brings neither "certitude, nor peace, nor help for pain," if the best consolation we can offer bereaved hearts is the assurance that though persons may perish ideals live on; if there is no positive evidence nor any sufficient ground of faith upon which we can rely; then few will there be who can realize this fact, with all its implications for human thought and feeling, without regret. In the words of G. L. Dickinson, "Life here would have *infinitely more value* if we knew that beyond death we should pursue, and ultimately to a successful issue, the elusive ideal of which we are always in quest. The conception that death ends all does not empty life of its worth, but it destroys, in my judgment, its most precious element, that which transfigures all the rest: it obliterates the gleam in the snow, the planet in the east; it shuts off the great adventure beyond death."

§

We cannot of course assume that without faith in immortality all is lost for the higher life of man, for his ethical and esthetic nature. That nature has sometimes triumphed on slim fare and with scant encouragements, as is proved alike by the history of ancient Stoicism and the prophetic religion of the Old Testament. But with Christianity the case is different. What is there left of the Christian view of life, of the Christian

ethic, of the Christian faith in God and divine revelation and the salvation of man, if faith in eternal life
must be given up? Other great historical religions, it
is true, have suffered the amputation of vital parts of
their original structure—or, equally significant, have had
vital parts grafted on—and have survived. In fact
Christianity itself early abandoned vital factors in its
primitive view of the world (for example, the Jewish-
Christian eschatology) without ceasing its growth and
progress or losing its significance for the spiritual life
of mankind: indeed, in the instance just cited, the
abandonment of chiliasm ("millenarianism") and of
popular Jewish eschatology released our religion from
an increasingly unsupportable burden and set it free
to take up its world-task. But could it abandon belief
in immortality and still have a message for the human
soul? Could it promise a more abundant life and at
the same time admit that for aught we know death must
end all manifestations and activities of life? For Christianity, the situation is crucial. If in this life we have
nothing more than a hope, a hope that seems less and
less justifiable and ever more completely out of place
in the world-view of modern thought, then Christianity
must retreat, "to the breath of the night-wind," and
forsake its claim to reveal the Way and the Truth. The
Christian religion stands or falls with its doctrine of
eternal life; there can be no compromise. The form
of the doctrine may vary; the conceptions which Chris-

tians in other ages have entertained regarding the life of the world to come, the peripheral adumbrations with which religious tradition has arrayed this central hope, may not be adequate; but the doctrine itself, the essential faith that men in and through Christ survive and conquer death, cannot be yielded and Christianity continue. It would be like the amputation of a man's head; feet, hands and a few other organs he can part with if he must; but not this.

It is a situation unique in Christian history when the Church is required to defend the faith in immortality. In earlier ages this could be taken for granted. In the days of Jesus, it is quite certain that the majority of his Jewish contemporaries explicitly held the doctrine. His apostles found the wide Graeco-Roman world permeated with popular cults and religious philosophies whose chief principle was immortality. The good news of the Gospel found eager listeners; it told men how to make certain of the life to come, for which they already longed, now that "the kindness of God our Saviour and his love toward man" had appeared. Christ had "brought life and immortality to light"; he offered men that explicit assurance of its reality which they had always craved. All through the long struggle of the early centuries, the Church's message was eagerly welcomed by those whose antecedent and inherited faiths and fears had bred in them the deep longing for divine salvation in another world. Down even to the days of

Paley and Butler, immortality could be assumed as a basic factor in "natural religion"; the Christian revelation cast a flood of fresh light upon a hope already firmly fixed in the human heart; indeed, the very firmness and universality of that hope could be viewed as a priori evidence in support of its final fulfillment in "the Christian scheme." But today, as with the miracles of the Bible, which were once "evidential" but now offer difficult problems for the conscientious Christian thinker, the center of gravity has shifted, and eternal life itself must be proved. Man's immortality is no longer proof of the goodness of his Creator; instead, the goodness of the Creator must—if possible—be urged as one reason for assuming that man in some measure shares His eternity. With the Psalmist of the Old Testament, the theist of today may say,

> *Thou* wilt not leave my soul in Sheôl.

His faith in God supports, it is not supported by, his faith in human immortality. Hence in order to maintain its front line of advance the Christian Church finds it necessary to take over the task once accomplished by cults and philosophies and the "natural religions" of the race, and to prove again, if possible, the everlasting hope. Its first task is to encourage men to look upon themselves as destined for a higher and better world, as born to live forever, as potential citizens of heaven.

I

The Christian Belief in Immortality

THE world in which Christianity arose was very generally convinced of man's survival of death. There were certain exclusive circles in which this was doubted or denied, such as the Stoic and Epicurean schools of philosophy in the Graeco-Roman world and the Sadducees among the Jews; but popular feeling had retained from primitive times the belief in some kind of immortality which was to be man's lot after death. It was therefore unnecessary, as a rule, for the new religion to persuade men to belief in an after-life before urging its other claims upon faith. The Gospel came, rather, as a revelation of the way, divinely manifest, to happiness and salvation in the world to come: salvation "in Christ," the foretaste of which was a redeemed ethical and spiritual life in the present. In place of fears and misgivings for the future, Christianity brought men an assurance of hope, a "true word" about the future, and a pledge of eternal happiness to those who accepted Christ as their Lord.

§

Various factors had contributed to this popular belief in immortality. In Palestine, the two centuries before the birth of Christ saw the rise of faith in a happy personal immortality for the righteous.

The old and probably primitive Hebrew conception of the after-life is classically expressed in the Old Testament:

> The dead praise not thee, O Yahweh,
> Neither all they that go down into Sheôl;
> The living, the living, he shall praise thee.

The author of the Book of Job shares the same view. "If a man die, shall he yet live?"

> Man dieth, and is laid low:
> Yea, man giveth up the ghost, and where is he?
> As the waters fail from the sea,
> And the river wasteth and drieth up,
> So man lieth down and riseth not;
> Till the heavens be no more, they shall not awake,
> Nor be roused out of their sleep.

The Old Testament conception of Sheôl, as the place of the departed, is that of an underground cavern, remote from the sphere of Yahweh's influence. From it may arise, if successfully conjured, the spirits of the dead, like Samuel at the call of the witch of Endor. But the necromancer was a disturber of their peace; perhaps the sight of the familiar upper world of sunlight and of living human beings revived in them sad longings and regrets at their banishment. Even in the Book of Job, which modern scholars date variously in the fifth, fourth, or third centuries before Christ, the problem of human suffering finds no solution in a compensating life of happiness after death; and whoever wrote its epilogue, whether the author or a later editor, the great tragedy becomes in the end only a trial of faith, permitted by an infinitely wise God whose ways are beyond searching and whose paths are past finding out. How nearly the book approached to the later solution, compensation in a life to come, is clear from the chapter already quoted:

> Oh, that thou wouldest hide me in Sheôl,
> That thou wouldest keep me secret, until thy wrath be past,
> That thou wouldest appoint a set time, and remember me
> . . .
> All the days of my warfare would I wait,
>   Till my release should come.
> Thou shouldest call, and I would answer thee:
> Thou wouldest have a desire to the work of thy hands.

The hope is there, the eager yearning for Yahweh's goodness and mercy to be revealed after death; but it proves too good to be true, a heaven for earth too high, and the seer falls back upon the old animistic notion of persistence in Sheôl, without knowledge or love or hope.

> So thou destroyest the hope of man;
> Thou prevailest for ever against him, and he passeth . . .
> His sons come to honor, and he knoweth it not.

This may be taken as the highest expression of the general Old Testament tradition prior to the second century before Christ. There were variations from this view, particularly where Judaism came under the influence of Greek or Persian speculation; as in Ecclesiastes, where it is maintained that "the dust returns to the earth as it was, and the spirit to God who gave it"; or as in the later Alexandrian apocryphal work, The Wisdom of Solomon, which even goes so far as to suggest a belief in preëxistence, and insists that

> The souls of the righteous are in the hand of God,
> And no torment shall touch them . . . .
> Because God made trial of them, and found them worthy of
>   himself . . . .
> They shall judge nations, and have dominion over peoples;
> And the Lord shall reign over them for evermore.

Yet here too the older beliefs survive, as in the passage,

> In the memory of virtue is immortality,
> Because it is recognized both before God and before men.

The crux of the problem, for the writers of the Old Testament, lay in the difficulty of conceiving any other mode of existence after death than that which primitive thought supplied. Unlike the history of Greek speculation, the rise of ethical and spiritual religion in Palestine was unattended by any development in philosophy or psychology. The ethical and religious concepts of prophets and seers had still to be wrought out in the formulas of every-day language. The "soul" was the principle of life in man, which differentiated him from inanimate objects and from the beasts that perish. It entered him at birth, or before (the precise moment of psychic animation seems not to have been discussed), and its survival in Sheôl was no different in kind from that anticipated by almost all early peoples—a form of existence suggested, no doubt, alike by the custom of burial and by the experience of dreams. The term "spirit" occurs in the Old Testament, it is true; but there is no consistent trichotomy in Hebrew thought. The two conceptions were generally fused, as in the passage in Genesis: "And Yahweh Elohim formed man of the dust of the ground, and breathed into his nostrils the breath of life (*n'shamah*, a word frequently used for 'spirit'); and man became a living soul (*nephesh*, the animal soul)." The more specific term, *ruach* ("spirit," or "wind"), was frequently reserved for the higher intellectual or emotional qualities, as in "the spirit of understanding," "to revive the spirit of the humble," "the Spirit of God"—though here again no restricted meaning was attached to the term. Lacking, then, a consistent terminology, a fact which frequently adds to the difficulties of interpretation, it is no cause for wonder that the Old Testament writers found no concept ready at hand which might suggest a mode of survival different from that proposed by primitive animism.

§

However, the pressure of experience and the changes effected by great crises in national life often force upon men new ideas and inspire hopes hitherto undreamt. Two important factors served to make concrete and vivid the Jewish belief in personal immortality during the period preceding the rise of Christianity: the influence of other religions, and the martyrdoms under Antiochus.

Following the conquests of Alexander the Great in the Near East, a new and cosmopolitan world of thought, religion, and political organization came to pass. The older national and municipal religions of Egypt, Persia and Syria were swept into a common melting-pot, whose final product—when other religions and philosophies had been added—became in the course of several centuries the "syncretism" of Roman days. Almost unique in its isolation, the Jewish religion refused to be absorbed in this syncretizing process. It maintained its ancient purity, refusing to identify the God of the fathers with the "Zeus of Many Names" whom the surrounding peoples now worshipped. At the same time, ideas too subtle for rigorous exclusion crept in and modified the common conceptions of the soul, the after-life, the judgment, the fate of the individual, matters upon which traditional Judaism possessed no rigid dogmas. The Greek influence is already apparent in some of the later Old Testament writings, such as Ecclesiastes and certain of the Psalms which preceded in date the time of Antiochus IV. The chief point of contact, however, was probably in Egypt, where large numbers of Jews were colonized, whose loyalty to the ancestral religion was as indisputable as their growing affiliation with Hellenism. Still another outside influence, though one harder to trace, came from the religion of Persia. By what mediation it reached the Jews of Palestine is difficult to determine, though very likely the large branch of the Diaspora colonized in Babylonia should be remembered in this connection. Its influence affected the conceptions of the after-life in a way more closely germane to Jewish thought than was that of Graeco-Roman syncretism. No rigid definition is possible; but it may probably be fairly stated that Greek influence provided the conception of spiritual immortality, the survival of the disembodied soul, a conception indigenous to Egyptian thought; while the Persian or Mazdaean conceptions of the future resurrection, judgment, heaven and hell made concrete and explicit ideas which had long been latent in Hebrew thought. The inherited doctrine of "the Day of Yahweh," when the nations should be judged and Israel receive its just deserts, was identified with the doctrine of a Last Judgment wherein individuals should receive reward or punishment for their deeds, the righteous in a terrestrial paradise of delight, the wicked in torments of hell. With this was readily combined the idea of resurrection, i.e. the reanimation of their dead bodies— the righteous that they might enjoy an age of bliss of variously estimated duration, the wicked in order to be made to feel the pains of hell.

The final factor in producing the pre-Christian Jewish eschatology was not, however, the infiltration of such popular conceptions; it was the agonizing experience of persecution and martyrdom under the Seleucid emperor, just preceding the revolt of the Maccabees and during the early stages of the war for independence. Antiochus had determined to Hellenize the Jewish nation, and thus render more loyal the southern province of his domain as a bulwark against the Ptolemies of Egypt. The record of this effort and of its failure is to be read in the Books of the Maccabees; but the profoundest expression of its result upon Jewish thought is the prophetic Book of Daniel. The majority of modern scholars agree in dating this work at about the year 165 B.C.—at the very beginning of the revolt and before its success was assured. It was a patriotic manifesto, in one sense, a word of encouragement in days of darkness and uncertainty. It assured the struggling patriots under Mattathias and his sons, fighting their desperate battle of the wilderness, that God was still supreme, and would soon destroy the power that opposed them. "And the kingdom and the dominion, and the greatness of the kingdoms under the whole heaven, shall be given to the people of the saints of the Most High." World-empire was Israel's destiny! But what of those who had already fallen? What reward should be theirs whose blood had been shed in defense of the sacred Law and of the holy city of God?   Would God forget them when His day arrived and the kingdom of this world became the possession of His people for ever?   This was an impossible supposition.   "Many of them that sleep in the dust of the earth shall awake, some to everlasting life, and some to shame and everlasting contempt.   And they that are wise shall shine as the brightness of the firmament; and they that turn many to righteousness as the stars for ever and ever."   It is difficult to determine precisely the form in which this promise is visualized, a difficulty which is only natural in dealing with an apocalyptic writing like the Book of Daniel.   It is a resurrection, to glory or to shame, not a survival in a spiritual Beyond that is contemplated; and the future life has no end—the resurrection is unto "everlasting" life or contempt.   But it is to be noted as a fact of first importance that this hope had its rise in the demand for justice—to martyr and to traitor—a justice whose realization the circumstances of the present forbid.

The contrast between this view of life and destiny and that which elsewhere in the Old Testament is accepted without question (or questioned, as in Job, only to be accepted) is too great to be overlooked.   In the Book of Daniel the righteous and unrighteous simply do not receive their reward in this life, either in prosperity and length of days or their opposite.   The only prospect of a final apportioning of deserts is in the life to come, af-

ter the resurrection.   Thus a new view of human life
and destiny enters Jewish thought. Persecution and
martyrdom have brought it forth, and it clothes itself
in popular conceptions derived partly from primitive
Semitic animism, partly from a more highly developed
system of eschatology, either Persian or Babylonian.

§

From this time, that is from the early part of the second century before Christ, belief in a resurrection and
judgment—at least of the conspicuously faithful or un-
faithful who have not received their reward in this life—
remains an integral part of Jewish religious thought.
Its great elaboration in the apocalyptic and pseudepi-
graphic literature of the following centuries attests its
popularity and wide diffusion.   Lacking dogmatic control or refusing to accept the restraints of orthodox tradition and the dictation of the conservative Sadducaean
hierarchy, the belief gradually permeated almost the
whole structure of Jewish religion.   The popular lay-
teachers of Judaism, the Pharisees, lent it their ready
support; certain sections of the apocalyptic literature are
almost certainly their work.   The scribes, the author-
ized expounders of the Law, were not greatly concerned
to dispute it; there was little in the Torah either to
countenance or to disprove it; if anything, such a doctrine reenforced the claims of the Law and supplied
additional motives for its scrupulous observance.   Only

the Sadducees, who contented themselves with the letter of the Mosaic Law and were not concerned with contemporary religious movements, remained aloof and uninfluenced by the belief. In the New Testament they are credited with maintaining that "there is no resurrection, neither angel, nor spirit." They possibly looked upon the whole body of popular eschatology as a pagan superstition; its appeal was not to the Law, for it claimed as its authority the private visions of seers. Educated Sadducees may have seen through the mantle of pseudonymous authorship and discredited the attachment of a venerated ancient name to the ecstatic or poetic writing of a contemporary—as in the purported writings of Enoch, the Twelve Patriarchs, Noah, and others. It was a technical victory when Jesus pointed out to the Sadducees that the Law itself taught the survival—and therefore the implied resurrection—of the dead.

In the teaching of Jesus, immortality is not so much affirmed as taken for granted. The popular belief in a life to come made this possible. It also provided the common vehicle of language in which his teaching could be set forth. The form in which the future life of the blessed was conceived was "the Kingdom of God." Immortality, i.e. resurrection, was an inevitable connotation of this hope for most of Christ's hearers, and belonged to a wide group of ideas and expectations in popular religious thought—the Messiah, the Judgment, the restoration of Israel, the bliss of the righteous and the penalties of the wicked. Without the physical resurrection, these items in the future world-program were either impossible or realizable only in a very limited way. For popular thought in Palestine still made nothing of the conception of the disembodied soul, familiar to Greek speculation and to at least a considerable part of Graeco-Jewish thought outside Palestine.

The beginning of Jesus' preaching in Galilee was the announcement, "The Kingdom of God is at hand." John the Baptizer had already appeared as the divinely commissioned herald of the coming Day of Judgment, and the immediate inference was that the Messiah was about to appear. In the Judgment which would presently be held, not only nations but also individuals were to receive their just due. This much of the popular belief, now grown tense with expectation as the result of John's preaching, Jesus shared and took for granted in his own ministry. "Now after John was delivered up, Jesus came into Galilee, preaching the Gospel of God, and saying, 'The time is fulfilled, and the Kingdom of God is at hand; repent and believe in the Gospel.'" But whereas the majority of his hearers were intent upon the outward form of the coming Kingdom and upon their privileges as its future citizens, his real message was one of repentance and faith. Much more was required than mere descent from Abraham to ensure one's entrance into life. "Many shall come from the east and the west, and shall sit down with Abraham and Isaac and Jacob in the Kingdom of Heaven; but the sons of the Kingdom shall be cast forth into outer darkness." What God demands is ethical purity, a righteousness of inner motive exceeding the legal and external righteousness of the scribes and Pharisees, uprightness in the secret sight of God, unassuming humility, gentleness, the will to peace, simple, unsophisticated goodness like that of a little child, love and mercy and the self-dissatisfied thirst for true righteousness: these were the virtues Christ stressed in describing the character pleasing to God and required of those who were to be subjects of the coming Kingdom.

This illustrates the emphasis which our Lord laid upon men's preparation for entrance into the Kingdom, rather than upon the certainty of its coming (which he and his hearers assumed), or the precise form it should take, or its date. Such questions of form and date he laid aside as of less consequence: "It is not for you to know the times or the seasons, which the Father hath set within his own authority"; "of that day or that hour knoweth no man"; "the Kingdom cometh not with observation." Jesus was no apocalyptic visionary or enthusiast. So remote were the interests and anxieties of some of his contemporaries, to which concern over the future had given rise, that he counselled his disciples to ignore them. "Fear not, little flock; it is your Father's good pleasure to give you the Kingdom." Anxious

thought he forbade, though at the same time he rebuked
the careless indifference of the man who laid up treasure
on earth but was not "rich towards God."   It is impossible to exaggerate the calm certainty with which he
faced the future, in the very midst of overwhelming disappointments of his own, and proclaimed with confidence the will of God, even though the "signs of the
times" pointed to a far different denouement of his
career than that popularly expected for the Messiah.
This unfailing certainty was expressed in such words as
those in the Gospel of St. Matthew—words in which
some scholars have found the clue to his "Messianic
consciousness" and the explanation of his whole career
from baptism to crucifixion: "All things have been delivered unto me of my Father; . . . Come unto me,
all ye that labor and are heavy laden, and I will give
you rest.   Take my yoke upon you, and learn of me;
for I am meek and lowly in heart, and ye shall find rest
unto your souls.   For my yoke is easy, and my burden
is light."   Not a word here about the Messianic future,
or the life to come!   Yet one cannot but feel, in the
presence of such a spirit, that questions of life and death
and the final chapters of terrestrial history are really
irrelevant; they concern only the phenomenal and accidental, while here is the abiding and real.

Surprising as it may seem to the modern student of
Jesus' life and teaching, it is a fact that our Lord was
remarkably reticent upon the subject of the after-life.

The parable of Dives and Lazarus is after all only a "parable" (if it be not two parables in one), obviously symbolic in its phraseology: for example, the reference to Abraham's bosom—"whatever that be," as Augustine wrote after the death of his friend Nebridius. And the aim of the parable is not to portray future bliss or torment, but to urge the wisdom of numbering our days and applying ourselves to the duties of brotherhood and love now in this present time. The controversy with the Sadducees contains a certain amount of positive teaching: "When they shall rise from the dead, they neither marry, nor are given in marriage; but are as angels in heaven"—a saying which Luke considerably elaborates, partly in view of what follows this passage. In addition to this positive statement, there is the proof from the Law of the doctrine of resurrection: If God addresses Moses and describes himself as "the God of Abraham, Isaac, and Jacob," though the patriarchs were then dead, it is an error to suppose that the dead are not raised. "He is not the God of the dead, but of the living." To this statement St. Luke, who was a Gentile, adds, "For all live unto Him"—an interpretation which possibly misses the point of the implied *resurrection*, and substitutes the Greek conception of immortality in its place.

In the Fourth Gospel, which presents Jesus' teaching in a later form, to be dated most probably early in the second century, our Lord is represented as announcing the resurrection in so many words: "The dead shall hear the voice of the Son of God; and they that hear shall live. . . . All that are in the tombs shall hear his voice, and shall come forth; they that have done good, unto the resurrection of life; and they that have done ill, unto the resurrection of judgment." Even if these are not Jesus' authentic words—as many scholars now affirm—they doubtless go back to a very early stage in the primitive Christian tradition, and reflect the thought of the Church at a time very early in its history. Their Jewish coloring is all the more evident in a writing as strongly influenced by Hellenic mysticism as the Gospel of John. The same is true of the famous passage in the fourteenth chapter, "In my Father's house are many mansions," a conception which may be paralleled from the Book of Enoch and other Jewish writings. At the same time, the general tenor of the Fourth Gospel is upon another level, which, in spirit if not in form, is usually viewed as a fair interpretation of the teaching of Jesus. "I came that they might have life, and have it abundantly"; "If any man serve me, let him follow me; and where I am, there also shall my servant be"; "I am the Way and the Truth and the Life"; "I am the Resurrection and the Life"; "He that believeth on the Son hath eternal life"; "He that heareth my word, and believeth Him that sent me, hath eternal life, and cometh not into judgment, but hath passed out of death into life." It may not be necessary to suppose that the historical Jesus used these precise words in Galilee or Judea, words suggesting Hellenistic philosophy and mysticism; but they certainly do express the early Christian experience, under the guidance of Christ's influence and teaching—perhaps even as utterances of the exalted Christ through prophets in the early Church; and the attitude they reveal towards death and judgment and the after-life is much the same as that which the other gospels portray as our Lord's. His calm assurance, his simple unconcern over details of the future, his certainty of God, his own experience of communion with the Father—these are as clear from the Synoptic Gospels as from the Fourth. The Gospel of John views eternal life as an accomplished fact, something to be realized here and now and not only in the future. And this is precisely what the other gospels lead us to think was the way in which Jesus viewed it and experienced it—it is the whole theological presupposition of "realized eschatology."

This attitude of calm trust, of unconcern over external details, of rejoicing in a present experience whose reality is sufficient guarantee of its permanence, ought to be far more inspiring as an example to the Church than it has been in the past or is now. Anxiety was meaningless to our Lord. There is even a note of impatient scorn in his rebuke, "O ye of little faith!"—more tenderly translated by Dr. Moffatt in the words, "O men, how little you trust Him!" Details were only decorative; they possessed symbolic value but little more. Eternal life was a present fact, though not all men realized it. "I thank thee, Father, Lord of heaven and earth, that thou hast hid these things from the wise and understanding, and didst reveal them unto babes; yea, Father, for so it was well-pleasing in thy sight." Into the depths of the divine consciousness which these words imply we may not peer. "No one knoweth the Son, save the Father." No one knows what communings took place upon the lonely mountaintop, in the solitude of the "desert," or on the hillside in the dewy dawn, "a great while before it was day." Yet there, we may feel sure, lay the secret of his confidence and of his power. He could afford to neglect details, and ignore the interesting descriptions of heaven for which men always yearn, because he had that to give men which rendered those details secondary and negligible. His were "the words of eternal life."

There are, it is true, certain passages in which a materialistic, this-worldly conception of the Kingdom is implied, as in the promise to the disciples that they should "sit upon twelve thrones, judging the twelve tribes of Israel," or the vow at the last supper, "I will no more drink of the fruit of the vine until I drink it new with you in my Father's kingdom." It is true that sayings in which the Kingdom is viewed as a future consummation alternate with sayings which represent it as a present, spiritual reality. It is true that future rewards and punishments are assumed: "enter thou into the joy of thy lord"; "depart from me, ye cursed"; "without is darkness and wailing and gnashing of teeth"—phrases which are no doubt metaphorical but nevertheless imply future retribution. It is doubtful if historical or literary criticism entirely obliterate these traces from Jesus' teaching, even though it seems evident that the Gospel of Matthew has considerably heightened the "apocalyptic" coloring of many passages—as in the famous "Little Apocalypse" taken over from the thirteenth chapter of Mark. The early Christian tradition of Jesus' sayings was not unaffected by the thought, the emotional experiences and the eager expectations of the earliest generations of his followers: nevertheless, this element was not introduced as something wholly new into the Master's teaching, since practically all of the evangelic sources, even the oldest, reflect it. The truth appears to be that our Lord's human temperament was more mystical than critical. He was aware of the values, ethical and spiritual, in much of the current phraseology. He used it mainly in a symbolic and figurative sense. Hence he was not concerned to deny it; instead, he silently put aside its more materialistic implications and emphasized the truths which were of primary importance for men's salvation. This principle seems to be involved in all his teaching regarding the Kingdom of God, the resurrection and judgment,

Paradise, the future state, the eternal bearing of human choices, thoughts and deeds.

§

Even more significant than Jesus' teachings, for the early Christian belief in immortality, was his own resurrection from the dead. The meaning of Jesus' resurrection for the earliest disciples was, of course, inconceivable apart from his teaching and from the impression of his personality upon them, crystallized in their faith in his Messiahship. It was not just anyone's resurrection; it was the resurrection of *the Christ*. At the same time it was the experience of the risen Lord that translated hope into conviction and interpreted his teaching in the light of present fact. However our modern scientific theology or religious psychology may endeavor to explain the various appearances, there is no doubt whatever that actual experience lies back of the reports recorded in the New Testament. It may not be possible, on the basis of the data provided, to ascertain the sequence or precise form of the resurrection appearances. These data, from the earliest in time of writing, St. Paul's list in First Corinthians, to the latest, the Appendix to John and the fragments of the oldest apocryphal Gospels, cover a period of at least fifty years, perhaps a century; and the channels of tradition by which they were handed down, to St. Paul, to the writers of the Gospels or to their sources, are no longer ascertainable. But the whole course of the earliest Christian history as represented in the New Testament becomes meaningless if the resurrection appearances of Jesus are either ignored or explained away.

There are many persons who accept the statement of the creed, "On the third day he rose again," neither on the testimony of historical evidence nor as a matter of authority or of tradition, but out of a sense of congruity. Such a person as Jesus could not die. He and death are terms as incompatible as life and death, light and darkness. This was the feeling of the disciples themselves as echoed in the earliest record of the apostolic preaching: "It was impossible that death should hold *him*." But this must not lead us to assume that the disciples had expected Jesus to rise from the grave, and that out of this expectation arose the belief that he actually had risen. No fact of history is better attested than their discouragement and sense of defeat following the death of their Master. Up to the very last they had not taken seriously his repeated announcement (as stated in the gospels) of the fate which awaited him in Jerusalem. Somehow or other, they felt, he must be about to "restore the Kingdom to Israel," ascend a throne, and establish by miracle his sovereignty over the nations; somehow the arrival of the divine kingdom would prevent his death. The end had come as suddenly as it was unforeseen. Now that Jesus was dead, their cause was lost, and nothing remained for them but to go home and resume their fishing, sadder but wiser men —if disillusionment be wisdom. They had expected an earthly kingdom; Jesus' crucifixion was the most terrible blow which that kind of expectation could possibly receive. Then came the great experience of Easter morn. Their faith revived. Their conviction deepened to the martyr pitch. And the belief that Jesus was Messiah, in spite of all contrary outward conditions, during his earthly ministry, became the faith that Jesus was Messiah in spite of the greatest contradiction of all, his death. They could scarcely have believed that Jesus was Messiah after the resurrection unless they had already believed it, in some sense, before that event—the resurrection came as the divine confirmation of this belief. But they could scarcely have continued to believe in Jesus' Messiahship apart from the resurrection. Stupendous as the event appears to the mind of our scientific age, the belief in Christ's resurrection is absolutely required in order to explain the psychological process which lay back of the earliest manifestation of Christianity as a religious movement in Judaism in the first half of the first century. Some kind of experience of fellowship with Jesus after his death, a real and continuous relationship with him, sufficient to give them the overwhelming persuasion of his continued existence, and existence as Messiah, is indispensably necessary to account for it.

In the earliest apostolic preaching this fact was of

first importance. If Jesus was still alive after his passion, and had ascended in glory to the right hand of God, then it followed that Jesus' teaching concerning the Kingdom, including all that the disciples had been led by him to hope and expect, was divinely guaranteed. Christ was in heaven, soon to return. The outpoured Spirit had been sent by him, as the earnest of his coming; his own "mighty works" were continued through his apostles; the message of repentance, which had been his message from the beginning, was now urged with added force upon those who had neglected to "turn and repent" at their first calling. It was true that the Kingdom had not yet been set up and that the judgment had not yet taken place; but the present time was only an interval, presumably of short duration, a period of grace which had been granted to men in order that they might no longer neglect so great a salvation. Any day the Lord might appear "on the clouds of heaven." This "eschatological temper" of the early period in the Church's history, the high tension of expectancy which filled the hearts of believers, is sufficiently reflected in the New Testament. We find it not only in the early chapters of the Book of Acts but also, if in a less degree or in different form, in almost every other writing. The Apocalypse of John, whose present form seems to date from the reign of Domitian, proves the continued existence of this point of view; and the later "chiliasm" or millenarianism which survived into the fourth or fifth century, and has been revived repeatedly throughout Christian history, attests the vigor of this hope. In its light the early Christians interpreted and handed down the oral tradition of Jesus' teaching, and then continued to read and expound it after it had been written down in the gospels. It was in the light of apostolic experience that they understood their own hope of resurrection and exaltation.

§

Without venturing too far into the field of New Testament criticism, which it is not the purpose of this volume to undertake, it may be said that the earliest accounts of the resurrection appearances of our Lord indicate a more spiritual mode of manifestation than the later. St. Paul's list includes his own "heavenly vision" on the way to Damascus—certainly a different kind of appearance than those in which the risen Lord is said to have partaken of broiled fish, or bade Thomas place his hand in Christ's side, or said, "Handle me and see, for a spirit hath not flesh and bone, as ye behold me having." Emphasis upon physical reality was a perfectly natural tendency for later tradition to take; indeed, this was the only sense in which reality was understood by most men in ancient (as in modern) times. There was no popular knowledge of science, no criticism, no psychology, and little or no differentiation between realities apparent to the mind and those which might be ascertained by the evidence of the senses. There was no widespread criticism of religious experience, such as meets us everywhere today.

For St. Paul, on the other hand, a man whose religion was deep and intense and whose theology was rooted in experience, the vision of the risen and ascended Christ was determinative for his whole view of the after-life. He could refer to his conversion experience as God's "revelation of his Son in me"; and he could ex-hort his readers, "If ye then be risen with Christ, seek those things that are above, where Christ sitteth at the right hand of God." We must not assume that the fact of the physical resurrection was without significance for St. Paul. That fact was equally as real as the fact of the cross: "It was Christ who suffered, yea, who died and was buried, who rose again." But the risen life of Christ was a reality of a different order. "Christ being raised from the dead dieth no more: death hath no more do-minion over him." The body of the risen Lord is a "spiritual body." The mystical realism of his language involves no contradiction. The body of flesh, corrup-tible and subject to death, is "raised incorruptible" and "changed." For "this mortal must put on immortal-ity," since "flesh and blood cannot inherit the Kingdom of God, nor corruption inherit incorruption." The believer could be, and indeed was, a member of the spiritual "body" of Christ, deriving his life from the spiritual Source of new life. Christ was "the head of his body, the Church," and it was from the Head that its life was derived. The believer could be "present with the Lord" and in communication with him, even in this life. For this very reason, the Christian looked forward to a risen life of his own, beyond death, beyond the general resurrection, the pledge and guarantee of which was his real spiritual contact with the risen Lord here and now.

The manner in which the contradiction is overcome is described as fully as human language will permit in Paul's famous fifteenth chapter of First Corinthians, already quoted. The passage is not a section in systematic theology but, like the rest of the epistle, is hortatory and apologetic. Its aim is first to prove the reality and then to argue by analogy the possibility of Christ's resurrection, and to assert its significance for the common Christian hope. "If there is no resurrection of the dead [as some among you affirm], neither has Christ been raised; and if Christ has not been raised, then our preaching is void, and your faith is void—yes, and we are found false witnesses of God." The traditional Jewish conception of the resurrection is fully assumed; "the trumpet shall sound, and the dead shall be raised incorruptible, and we shall be changed." It is not a "spiritual resurrection" in the modern sense, the "resurrection" of the surviving soul, which would have been meaningless for St. Paul. It is, rather, a real transformation of the physical body into the spiritual body after the analogy of the "raising" of a kernel of wheat. The seed is sown and "dies," but the new stalk and its kernels are still the old grain transformed, raised to a new mode of existence. The life of the seed is continuous, and "God giveth it a body"; nevertheless, the two modes of existence are clearly distinguishable. So likewise, "if there is a natural body, there is also a spiritual body." A further analogy is adduced from the story of creation, in which Adam became a living soul; to this is added the fact of Christ's resurrection as "the last Adam," who is "a life-giving spirit." Christ's work is the creation of a new world, a new mode of existence, into which his followers and believers enter through union with him, a mode of existence which is to be permanent and everlasting and beyond the reach of corruption. "The first man is from the earth, earthy; the second man is from heaven. And as is the earthy, such are they also that are earthy; and as is the heavenly, such are they also that are heavenly. And as we have borne the image of the earthy [i.e. by descent from Adam], we shall also bear the image of the heavenly," through union with Christ, partaking of his triumphant life, sharing his resurrection.

Not only in this classical passage but elsewhere in his epistles St. Paul takes for granted the common expectation of the end of the age, the resurrection of both saints and sinners, the Messianic judgment, the establishment of the Kingdom, the permanent bliss of the

saved and the punishment of the wicked. At the same
time he was not particularly interested in the external
details of the "last things." Like his Lord, he placed
more emphasis upon ethical and spiritual values in
present experience. The outlook of the Christian life
was eschatological, for St. Paul as for his readers. The
background and framework of Christian thought were
supplied by apocalyptic theories and expectations, much
as for many modern minds the idea of universal progress
forms the background of all their thinking. At the
same time, passages occur like the following, in which
the apocalyptic outlook is no longer dominant: "We
know that if the earthly house of our tabernacle be dis-
solved, we have a building from God, a house not made
with hands, eternal in the heavens." Such a passage
could easily be interpreted without reference to the
eschatology of Messianism and wholly in terms of current Alexandrian Platonism. Nevertheless, the apocalyptic element is really present, as not only the context
but also Paul's other utterances imply. It is immediately followed by a passage in which the condition of
the "naked" soul, "unclothed" by its "habitation from
heaven," is pictured as a state of misery and distress.
Take such an utterance as this: "We all, with unveiled
face reflecting as a mirror the glory of the Lord, are
transformed into the same image from glory to glory,
even as from the Lord the Spirit." In this characteristic passage, which marks the culmination of his ethical

and mystical idealism and their fusion, the background
of thought is the apocalyptic vision of the risen Lord;
but the thought is certainly written out of the heart of
personal experience, and the values which it presupposes wholly transcend the apocalyptic-eschatological
scheme.   Eschatology, for St. Paul as for our Lord, was
"a medium for the exposition of a genuine spiritual life,
which did not rise and fall with any particular forecast
of the future."

§

In the remaining literature of the New Testament,
the Johannine writings form the larger and more significant part.   The Apocalypse, which is perhaps to a
considerable extent a recasting of older Jewish or Jewish
Christian material, reflects a time of persecution.   In
certain passages the author seems to despair of the
Church's continuance in this world; it is to be destroyed
root and branch, and only in the other world are the
saints to find peace.   The elaborate pictures of the coming woes, the judgment, the millennial Kingdom, the
final Consummation, are painted in colors clearly derived from Jewish apocalyptic.   But by this time, however, a Christian apocalyptic was developing, whose
chief distinction from its parent was the identification
of the Messiah with Jesus the Lord, and the saints and
martyrs with the persecuted Church.   It is as a classic
example of this type of thought that our New Testa-

ment Apocalypse, "the Revelation of St. John," should be considered. Though its influence has been incalculable through the Christian centuries, since it has been looked upon as a guidebook to heaven by countless readers, still the specifically Christian element in it is somewhat obscured by its involved symbolism and its naive expectation of divine vengeance upon the persecutors of the faithful. The conception of future bliss is the traditional Jewish one, for the most part, with added Christian features. Its heaven is one in which there is "no more curse; and the throne of God and of the Lamb shall be therein; and his servants shall do him service, and they shall see his face; and his name shall be on their foreheads. And there shall be night no more; and they need no light of lamp, neither light of sun; for the Lord God shall give them light; and they shall reign for ever and ever."

We can imagine what this book meant to those who first read it and pondered its visions and oracles. What consolation, what encouragement, what strength of soul it must have given brave and faithful believers, to whom tomorrow might bring the prefect and the warrant! We well know what it meant to later generations, to the mediaeval Church with its hymns, "O heavenly Jerusalem," "Light's abode, celestial Salem"; and to more modern Christians as well, for whom it has been almost the sole satisfaction of that well-nigh insatiable longing for a concrete, definite picture of the other world, a longing that is ever with us and that deepens to pathos in hours of bereavement. Nevertheless, it must be admitted that the pictures in the Book of Revelation are too concrete, too explicit, too elaborately imagined, and suggest too strongly the suspicion that they arose from repressed longings and earthly disappointments. The revulsion of feeling in our day against "the old-fashioned heaven and hell" may be laid at the door of the too-literal understanding of a book which, in at least some of its parts, we may believe was, for all its general symbolism, quite literally meant.

The Johannine Epistles, like the Fourth Gospel, and possibly like it showing traces of the influence of St. Paul, assume the eschatological outlook, but at the same time are vastly more concerned with present spiritual life. This life is, so to speak, *already* eternal, and its experience is ethically conditioned throughout. "We know that we have passed out of death into life, because we love the brethren!" There is little immediate danger of persecution, such as there was at the time the Apocalypse appeared. Nor are the readers exhorted, as are those of First Peter and the Epistle to Hebrews, to "abstain, as sojourners and pilgrims" from the gross sins of the flesh, or to "seek a better country, that is a heavenly"; instead, "these things have I written unto you, that ye may know that ye have eternal life, . . . ye who believe on the name of the Son of God." This lofty strain reaches its climax in the First

Epistle: "Behold what manner of love the Father hath bestowed upon us, that we should be called the children of God; and such we are."   Here we find a conception whose meaning in no wise depends upon any program of eschatology, though eschatology is sublimated, much after the manner of St. Paul, in what follows: "Beloved, now are we the children of God, and it is not yet made manifest what we shall be. We know that, when he shall appear, we shall be like him, for we shall see him even as he is.   And every one that hath this hope purifieth himself, even as he is pure."

§

As we turn from the New Testament to the writings of the second and following centuries, we note at once the continuity of thought and ideas, linking the Christian tradition with the New Testament, and through the New Testament with pre-Christian Judaism. As time went on and the sacred writings were gathered into a definitive, canonical collection, they exerted an increasingly normative influence. The principle of interpretation, as a rule, was to prefer a literal to a figurative meaning; or where both were possible, to make the literal meaning primary. Some contact with popular Judaism was maintained for a time, as may be seen in the fragments of Papias and in certain of the apocalypses. These contain passages which picture the future bliss as a time of renewed and supernatural fruit-fulness of the earth and a decidedly material prosperity for the elect. The chief examples of this literal inter-pretation are to be seen in Millenarianism and Mon-tanism, the former of which was strongly combatted by Origen and his school, while the latter soon fell into disrepute as a heresy and so lost influence.

Heathen conceptions had some part in moulding popular beliefs, brought into the Church, no doubt, by the Gentile converts. We find, for example, the idea of Tartarus—the very name occurs more than once in early Christian literature. At the same time, it is not difficult to imagine the sense of release and assurance which early Christianity, with its central doctrine of Jesus' resurrection, brought to the ancient Graeco-Roman world. In place of a sad hopelessness, of in-soluble doubt and grave forebodings, Christianity gave men a new confidence in the goodness of God, in the reality and desirableness of the after-life now conceived afresh by the Christians, which was certainly a new thing for the majority of pagans. It not only promised something for the future, it actually gave something here and now—a sense of freedom from fear (far differ-ent from that which Epicurus and Lucretius had offered men in atheistic materialism!), and an assurance of per-sonal moral triumph in Christ. Almost the best that pagan religion or philosophy apart from the mysteries had to offer at that time is summed up in the famous lines of Virgil,

> Felix qui potuit rerum cognoscere causas
> Atque metus omnis et inexorabile fatum
> Subiecit pedibus strepitumque acherontis avari.

"Happy is he who is able to recognize the causes of things, and has trampled under foot all fear, and inexorable Fate, and the rumblings of hungry Acheron!" But Christianity was something quite different from this in attitude, in spirit, in actual feeling—a substantial, psychological fact. The change which Christianity made is vividly recorded in the epitaphs. The *vixit* (he lived) of traditional pagan piety becomes the *vivit* (he lives) of Christian conviction. What the mystery religions and the ethical philosophies of the Hellenistic-Roman world could not actually furnish, but left men dimly longing for, Christ had already given his own. "We are more than conquerors through him who loved us." "Neither death, nor life, nor angels, nor principalities, nor things present, nor things to come, nor powers, nor height, nor depth, nor any other creature, shall be able to separate us from the love of God, which is in Christ Jesus our Lord." Here was a new force at work in the religious history of the Mediterranean world and of mankind generally.

The Christian apologists castigated the folly of heathen beliefs and rites, though they somewhat weakened

their arguments by asserting that the Greek philosophers borrowed their wisdom from the Old Testament.
Nevertheless, certain factors were present in the general
situation, gradually effecting a change in emphasis in
the Church's teaching, and destined to effect what was
in the end virtually a compromise with pagan thought.
The growth of the Church on Gentile soil by the admis-
sion of converts who brought with them the inherited
notions of the after-life; the spread of Oriental religions,
practically all of which taught an elaborate eschatology;
the effort of early Christian writers to systematize the
data of Old and New Testaments in the light of current beliefs—all these factors resulted in a growing synthesis of ideas. This synthesis in turn prepared the
way for the systematic scheme of cosmology and of future history, terrestrial and celestial, which the mediaeval Church elaborated and which supplied the foundation alike for the *Divina Commedia* of Dante and for
the *Summa Theologica* of Aquinas. It is somewhat
difficult to extract the positive Christian conception of
immortality from this body of traditional thought, this
system of ideas and beliefs, involving cosmology, an-
thropology, psychology, geology, Biblical interpretation,
classical lore—indeed, the subject matter of many of
the most modern of the sciences. The conception of
immortality was an integral part of the whole ecclesiastical view of human life and destiny, of the world's
history, the origin of the soul, the ethical requirements

of "the new Law," and the scheme of redemption. This world-view was largely undermined when Copernicus, Galileo, and their successors abolished the geocentric conception of the universe, and when modern astronomy, geology, chemistry, physiology, biology and psychology were born. The extent to which the traditional Christian view of immortality is rooted in the ancient patristic and mediaeval world-view is evident from the immense difficulty which Christians have experienced in conceiving the future apart from this traditional basis, at the behest of modern science. The time may of course come when the conception of immortality will be once more an integral part of a generally accepted scientific and philosophic world-view. But that time is not yet.

In the early period, i.e. in the second and third centuries, there was a tendency to define the resurrection of the "body"—St. Paul's consistent phrase—simply as *resurrectio carnis* (resurrection of the flesh), a tendency whose historical monument is the phrase in the Apostles' Creed. Though such writers as Justin, Athenagoras, Irenaeus, and Cyprian were ranged in opposition to the phrase, the fathers and apologists generally believed in the resuscitation of the very same body which man possessed while on earth—a circumstance which rendered their position less effective, though their motive was clearly to defend the fact of personal identity and to ensure the preservation of the whole of man's essential nature. The Alexandrian school forms the exception to this rule. Clement taught, in good Greek fashion, that the final goal of spiritual attainment was the deliverance of the soul from the fetters of the body, and he made use of current religious terminology in describing as "deification" the result of the gift of immortality. This was orthodox Platonic philosophy, in the second century if not orthodox Christianity. It was also popular Hellenistic mysticism. "Throughout the whole of Greek literature, from Homer downwards," as James Adam wrote in his *Vitality of Platonism,* "immortality was universally held to be an attribute of that which is divine: the 'immortal' is the 'uncreated.'" Suggestions of this idea are to be found even in parts of the New Testament (for example, in Second Peter). Clement's disciple Origen, however, endeavored to reinstate the simple doctrine of St. Paul, viz. that the spiritual body is organically continuous with the body of flesh but supplants it after the resurrection. If we lived in water, we should possess the bodies of fish; so likewise the heavenly state requires glorified bodies, like those of Moses and Elias and our Lord's own after his resurrection. Yet this spiritual body, as in the Pauline paradox, is both the same and not the same as the physical body which preceded it. Origen was apparently the first to expound the theory of continuity in terms of the molecular change within our mortal bodies. As our bodies today are identical with our bodies of twenty years ago, though every particle has changed, so the spiritual body is continuous with the earthly body. The "germinative principle," by which this identity is maintained throughout all change, he found in the soul, which "lays hold of fitting matter and shapes it into a habitation suited to its needs." "Into this condition [the spiritual body], then, we are to suppose that all this bodily substance of ours will be brought, when all things shall be reëstablished in a state of unity, and when God shall be all in all. And this result [i.e. the Consummation] must be understood as brought about, not suddenly but slowly and gradually . . . during the lapse of countless and unmeasured ages. . . . When therefore, all rational souls shall have been restored, . . . then the nature of this body of ours will undergo a change into the glory of a spiritual body." Origen's theology was condemned at several points, both in his own lifetime and later, and his "restorationism" has never been generally popular. But his influence was a mighty force to be reckoned with, and one which is by no means exhausted at the present time.

The final state of blessedness, according to the early fathers, is in communion with God and in company with Christ, with whom the saints reign in everlasting felicity. There is to be no toil, but an endless advancement in knowledge and in bliss, as "the elders" affirmed —so Irenaeus tells us—"through the Spirit to the Son, and through the Son to the Father." Clement of Alexandria figured the future life as an upward progress of the soul through seven heavens to rest in the "Ogdoad" —an eighth sphere, the final place of blessedness. Origen doubted if the Scripture warranted this Gnostic conception and gave preference to the idea suggested by the New Testament phrase, "aeons of aeons," as in the quotation above. "In that life of slow, vast progress, the soul is still free, is still tested by its use of freedom, rises and falls, is punished and rewarded according to its works." All punishment is remedial, in God's purpose. Rewards are not compensations, but "the full satisfaction of that restless love of truth which God has implanted in the soul," and not in vain. All revelation is gradual, here and hereafter, and the individual must coöperate in the process which is one of progress through discipline. The torments of "fire" are the burning pangs of conscience; the "outer darkness" is "banishment from Him who is the Light and the Life." Evil, being the creation of man—and of the devil—and not of God, cannot continue forever; indeed, its very nature, as Plato held, is negation, an absence of knowledge of the Good. Eternal does not, for Origen, mean "endless"; but, interpreting strictly the scripture phrase, "aeonian"; and even the "eternal sin" may finally be blotted out. He cannot quite conceive of final unrepentance, even in the most obdurate, after ages of disciplinary experience; and he insists that this life provides

only the narrowest basis for a judgment of the final
state of any soul. "Great is the truth, and it will pre-
vail, if it have but time to work in. Slowly yet certainly
the blessed change must come, the purifying fire must
eat up the dross and leave the pure gold." In the end,
as St. Paul had said, "All things shall be subject . . .
that God may be all in all."

In spite of Origen's condemnation, his theology exerted a profound and far-reaching influence upon later
times. It was the earliest and most original and, in
some respects, the most significant creative effort of the
Christian intellect in this field (as distinguished from
pure systematic traditionalism). The common belief
of the Middle Ages, and indeed the traditional teaching
of the Church on the subject of eschatology down almost
to the present, was a compromise between Origenism,
on the one hand, and, on the other, popular ideas derived partly from paganism but far more largely from
the Scriptures and from Jewish apocalyptic. The later
theologies of Augustine, Aquinas, and the Reformers,
and the later biblical Protestantism were more largely
concerned with other doctrines than eschatology; and
in so far as this compromise was altered, it was chiefly
by way of modification in the light of those other doctrines (for example, the Augustinian and Anselmic
doctrines of the Atonement), or by the reflection of
the Church's current practices. Moreover, no theology in Christian history more fully repays modern

study than that of the great Alexandrian Platonist. Origen was a pioneer, and some of his theories, as we have said, were later repudiated by the Church; but it was he who first mapped out the field, first carried to their full limits the philosophical implications of Christian experience and belief, first made theology a science.

§

Comprehension is characteristic of the genius of Catholicism—that is, of ancient historical Christianity. The great cardinal principles of "the faith" once affirmed, fully and unequivocally, the motto of further theological progress may almost seem to have been found in the text: "Gather up the fragments . . . that nothing be lost." A solid respect for spiritual experience, a willing reverence for all spiritual values, whencesoever derived, whether from Scripture or from the higher beliefs of paganism surviving in cultus or in pious custom, characterize not only the elaborate constructions of theological genius but the common beliefs of the great Church generally. Though sometimes at the cost of thorough consistency, this tendency really made possible the preservation of valuable but heterogeneous elements in the faith: a procedure not altogether irrational, considering the complexity and variety of the religious experience of mankind and of successive centuries of Christian life.

Broadly viewed, there is no doubt that the center of

interest has shifted more than once in the course of Christian history. The Apostolic Church viewed the present life as only an interval preceding the consummation and the Kingdom of God; individual immortality meant resurrection and future bliss or woe to follow the judgment. In the early Catholic Church, the Kingdom came to mean "Heaven," the supercelestial sphere of God, the angels and the saints; exclusion from the Kingdom meant "Hell"; and, under the influence of Greek thought, both popular and philosophical, the Intermediate State between death and the consummation came to be viewed as one of progressive purification. In the later Catholic and mediaeval Church, largely under the influence of St. Augustine, this temporary and progressive state came to be explicitly called "Purgatory." "I will not deny," says Augustine, "the existence of such a purifying fire, in the interval between the death of the body and that last day of judgment and retribution which shall follow the resurrection, which consumes the venial faults of worldliness: this I do not contradict, because possibly it is true." The passage is one which is considerably in debt to Origen, though it literalizes its original. The whole mediaeval view of life in this world as a preparation for a better one hereafter, already attainable in some measure through prayer and mortification whereby the pains of Purgatory are lessened, is continuous with the earlier view, if not with the New Testament teaching; but it was deeply colored by the economic and social conditions of the times, especially during the Dark Ages which followed the decline of classical culture.

With the arrival of the new dawn, and through the following period as the day advanced, there has been not only a shifting of interest but also, apparently, an actual decline of interest in the subject of the life to come. The modern social interpretation of the Gospel, though it is in large measure the product of today, is by no means without antecedents in the immediate past. Modern missions, social service, sanitation and hospitals, the anti-slavery movement, the various applications of Christian principles to industry—these, it is true, are of today and yesterday. But the political activities and interests of men following the rise of nationalism in Europe after the thirteenth century; the discovery of new lands, the growth of science, the spread of learning, the increase of population which followed the betterment of living conditions and the expansion of commerce and industry—all these factors had a direct bearing upon the views and beliefs of men regarding their future destiny, and effected a greater shifting of interest in theology itself than any which former ages had witnessed. The tradition was continuous, down to the fourteenth century; and in certain large areas, it is true, has been continuous since that time. Elsewhere, continuity has been less a matter of ecclesiastical authority, orthodoxy has been differently defined, and tradition

has been counterbalanced either by historical exegesis
or by philosophical speculation. Protestant teaching
in this department has been in general continuous with
that of the ancient Catholic Church, barring such teachings as, for example, that which the Thirty Nine Articles
stigmatize as "the Romish Doctrine concerning Purgatory, Pardons . . . and also Invocation of Saints."   At
the same time, it has given larger room for freedom of
thought and criticism, for private interpretation and
speculation, in the absence, or with the decline in authority, of dogmatic formulations.   Accordingly, such
beliefs as that in a second or continued probation after
death, in a universal restoration, in the annihilation of
the obdurately wicked, and in conditional immortality,
have been put forth from time to time in various Protestant circles.   In the Roman Church no opportunity
for such developments exists, as they are excluded by
the official definitions. Protestant freedom has also
permitted the appearance from time to time of enthu-
siastic sects, millenarian and other, reminding one of
the Montanists and chiliasts of the early Church.
Their contribution to thought upon the subject has
been chiefly a reënforcement of literal biblicism, and
few have long survived the variously anticipated dates
of the Second Advent. On the other hand, it is undeniable that modern Protestantism has tended to produce an identification of Christian theology with social
idealism or, more popularly, a general morality based

upon religion. We can scarcely deny that this tendency, as described by the late Dean Mathews, "has been to a large extent buttressed by that scepticism or agnosticism regarding individual immortality which marks modern thought. Such a situation has proved injurious to the spread of Christianity as more than a general ethical or religious system."

The rigidity of the Roman Catholic system of theology hardly antedates the Council of Trent and the Reformation period. On the other hand, modern Protestant laxity in doctrine is a development of recent years, though the germinal principle of Protestantism—freedom of biblical interpretation—involved also a certain doctrinal freedom from the start. It appears that the Reformation marked the sundering of two great forces, centripetal and centrifugal, which previously had balanced each other in a kind of equilibrium. The centripetal force became dominant in the Roman Church, which retained possession, very largely, of the earlier Christian heritage of tradition, sentiment, poetry, and customs enshrining men's age-long beliefs—an inheritance dating back to late classical times and the earliest beginnings of Latin Catholicism. In the Protestant Churches, the other force gained sway, and the problem of salvation and eternal life became a purely individual one; as defined by some of the early reformers, it depended upon membership in the body of the elect, not upon sacramental baptism or upon voluntary perseverance; and "blessed assurance" was either (psychologically viewed) the hard-won victory of the private soul or (theologically viewed) the free, unmerited gift of divine grace. The pre-Reformation Church was not ideal, in the thirteenth century or in any other "age of faith"; but as a public, social institution it was in some respects a more balanced, more adequate representative of the religion of Christ, a more effective teacher of idealism and of the genuinely spiritual perspective in which Christianity views human life, than either of the two major church groups, Roman and Protestant, that have succeeded it. In the days of its glory, the mediaeval Church was afflicted with neither hide-bound dogmatism nor paralyzing uncertainty and subjectivism.

§

We may conclude this chapter with a summary of the traditional teaching of the Church on the subject of immortality, before passing on to consider the belief in the light of modern science and speculation. Such a summary should represent not only the consensus of pre-Reformation Catholic teaching but also the more or less common beliefs of Protestantism—at least the doctrines presupposed in Protestant criticism. These doctrines may accordingly be taken, not unfairly, as a statement of the Christian belief in immortality.

1. According to traditional or orthodox Christianity,

the time of probation is limited to this present life. In spite of Origen's great contribution to the doctrine of the Intermediate State, his theory of future probation was generally rejected, not only on grounds of Scripture but also, it seems probable, on those of morality. It was a doctrine sure to be misunderstood by the simple. The tendency in the early Church to postpone baptism, due to the fear of a later lapse from the state of grace, was problem enough without offering an opportunity for repentance in the life to come.

2. At the same time, the vast majority of men, at the end of their time of probation, are as little prepared for the joys of heaven as they are deserving the pains of hell. The Intermediate State is therefore necessary for the further purification of the righteous, for the expiation of venial sins, and for the development, with the help of divine grace, of latent endowments of holiness or sanctity conferred by baptism and the other sacraments. This doctrine has been very largely ignored in popular modern Protestantism, most Protestants viewing the after-life as the immediate entrance of the soul into Heaven. Few, however, would deny the need for further progress in sanctification in heaven, even though it be in the presence of Christ in the midst of the celestial city. In the Roman Catholic Church, the doctrine of the Intermediate State has been formulated in terms of Purgatory, the fire in which "the souls of the holy," according to the Catechism of the Council of Trent,

"being disciplined for a fixed time, receive expiation, so that the way may be opened for them into the eternal country where nothing that is defiled may enter." This "fire" may often be too literally understood; yet such a view as that of St. Catherine of Genoa is not unique in the Roman Church. According to her teaching, the joy of the souls in Purgatory exceeds any that is possible on earth; and the sufferings in that state consist in bitter regret for the want of complete conformity to the divine will in the past, and in the realization of their present exclusion from the Beatific Vision. The sufferings of Dante's *Purgatory,* and of Cardinal Newman's *Dream of Gerontius,* like the joys, are those of an advancing spiritual state, not the crude pains of sense.

> There, motionless and happy in my pain,
>   Lone, not forlorn,—
> There will I sing my sad perpetual strain,
>   Until the morn.

3. The teaching of the New Testament and of the early Church, as seen for example in the Book of Revelation, that the departed live and are conscious and can pray for themselves and for others has been echoed throughout almost the whole of Christian history. A curious heresy which maintained "the sleep of the soul" until the general resurrection, though appealing to certain texts of Scripture and to the sentiments of many unimaginative Christians and pagans alike, as is evident from mortuary epitaphs, has never enjoyed great influ-

ence; and though revived from time to time it has been
repeatedly condemned by official action of the Church.
As far as it has been countenanced, it survives only in
such common expressions as "at rest" or "asleep in
Christ," which refer no doubt to the inanimate body
rather than to the active soul.   The general opinion of
the Church is far more accurately expressed in the words
of St. Jerome, "If the Apostles and Martyrs while still
in the body were able to pray for others when they still
ought to be full of care for themselves, how much more
can they do so after they have been crowned in victory
and triumph."   Official Protestantism has never sanc-
tioned the belief; but the common conception of the
after-life held among Protestants pictures that life as
one of activity, loving service, and fellowship with
Christ and others.   It is difficult to exclude prayer from
such a conception.

   4. That the eminently wicked, like the rich man in
the gospel parable, go at once to hell and suffer retribu-
tory punishments without hope of release or moderation
of torment has been commonly assumed.   This view
was consonant not only with the Jewish-Christian Scriptures and with the thought of classical paganism (as we
may see from the sixth book of the *Aeneid*), but also
with the emotions of the persecuted and oppressed.   It
was from such emotions that the conception no doubt
originally sprang.   *The Deaths of the Persecutors* was
a very popular book in the days of the Latin Fathers.

5. At the same time, the great saints were supposed to go at once to heaven where they were to attain and enjoy forever the immediate vision of God. St. Paul, for example, expressed the desire to "depart and be with Christ"—though he certainly expected the Consummation to take place in the immediate future. As a matter of religious experience, this sense of immediacy of access to God and to eternal bliss, and the deathbed or martyr visions of believers, perhaps support the inference—which a natural reverence would suggest—that these privileged ones should require no further waiting and separation from their Lord in the interval preceding the Consummation. Particularly in the early period, while the Church still lived under the constant threat of martyrdom, this feeling was widespread and strong. Dionysius of Alexandria wrote a letter, about the year 251, in which he describes the martyrs "now sitting with Christ and sharing in his Kingdom." Polycarp, Ignatius, Clement, and Tertullian also speak of the martyrs, as distinct from the rest of the faithful, in these terms.

6. At the end of the time of man's probation, which is likewise the end of the Intermediate State, Christ will return from heaven to earth "to judge both the quick and the dead." The bodies of all the departed, wicked and righteous alike, will be raised, and the bodies of the living "shall be changed." The divine judgment will be passed upon the "deeds done in the body," in this

present life; and all such deeds, and even "the thoughts in men's hearts," will be revealed. After the Judgment, the saved and the lost will be permanently separated and rewarded. How this affected those unprepared, by purgation, for the final state, was not determined. It is a logical difficulty, which shows the overlapping of the two ideas—one derived from primitive eschatology, the other from devout speculation.

This whole conception of "the last things," as we have seen, is largely derived from the biblical data, found in the New Testament and the Jewish apocalypses—the data which are formally systematized in the scheme just outlined. It was a perfectly definite, fairly consistent program of the end of all things. The extent of its influence upon the whole field of Christian thought is beyond calculation. Its authority is still undisputed in many quarters, and it remains the official theology over large areas of the Church. At no point in Christian thought, unless it be the orthodox doctrine of creation —with which this doctrine is in complete harmony and adjustment—have modern science and philosophy made faith more difficult at the present day.

7. As to the present state of the saved, very little is affirmed. The biblical data are scanty; we have noted our Lord's reticence and the general silence of the New Testament writers. According to St. John, "it has not yet been made manifest what we shall be." It is enough for the Christian soul to know that Heaven means the

vision of God and the everlasting presence of Christ, whose "servants shall serve him." The poetic embellishments of the idea in apocalypse or hymn, in poem or work of art, have generally been understood to be merely symbolic—like the New Testament "crown of righteousness." "Eye hath not seen nor ear heard, neither have entered into the heart of man, the things which God hath prepared for them that love him." But such positive hints as the Scriptures contain do imply that the life of heaven is active, devoted to the service of God, a life of fellowship, continence, endless blessedness and glory. "Blessed are the pure in heart, for they shall see God." It is a life of perfect attainment, in which longing is turned into enjoyment, the thirst for God into endless satisfaction. Even sins, as Dante teaches, will be no more remembered as sins, but only as facts, for the divine overruling shall have blotted out the sin, and out of evil brought forth good. Other religions have provided their followers with far more explicit descriptions of future bliss. Christianity has been, on the whole, decidedly reserved. It has provided enough, and no more than enough, positive teaching to assure men of safety and happiness and utter satisfaction in the highest realms of ethical and spiritual reality. We may really be thankful for this limitation. When we reflect upon the narrow limits of possible symbolism, and note the readiness of the human mind to literalize metaphor and exhaust its interest in the external ornamentation and detail of even the most august doctrines, when we consider the ease with which the human will fastens upon lesser ends than the highest and noblest and best, we are led to a thankful contentment with the few, simple, yet profound expressions with which divine revelation and the developing Christian consciousness have supplied us.

> This is all ye know . . .
> And all ye need to know.

8. The final state of the lost is generally viewed as one of banishment from God. Latin theologians have distinguished between a "pain of loss" and a "pain of sense," to both of which the condemned are subject; but both have been interpreted metaphorically. Origen, Ambrose, Jerome so understood the expressions in the Bible. Augustine, Aquinas, John of Damascus wavered, and later teachers often understood the fire of hell to be literal—which the doctrine of the physical resurrection, in fact, implied. Pain of sense would be impossible without the physical resurrection of the wicked.

Punishment has almost universally been viewed as unending. If man's free will is an actual fact and not a fiction, then the choice of evil, steadily and consciously and with full knowledge, can result in no other state than final identification with the evil which is loved and chosen. This teaching, though supported by Scripture, appears rather as a logical inference from man's freedom of choice and from the demands of the ethical imperative.   If the choice be wrong, i.e. sinful, it must be for ever wrong; and if a choice be final, it cannot afterwards be rescinded.

> No power can the impenitent absolve;
> Nor to repent and will at once consist,   _
> By contradiction absolute forbid.

At the same time, speculation among theologians rarely went the length of inquiring how many should be found in this state.   Apart from the biblical statements, it might be questioned whether any human soul should ever attain its destiny thus.   Some theologians have held that the pains of hell are mitigated in time; others have taught that none but the saved survive, the lost being annihilated; still others have maintained that all men everywhere, and the devil and his angels as well, shall finally be saved in "the times of the restoration of all things."   Such theories, though each has had its attractions for many Christians, have not won either general assent or official approbation.   They are not consonant with the biblical norm of the faith, nor are their implications consonant with the more fundamental principles of Christian theology and ethics.

"Revealed truth," says a modern theologian, "leaves unsolved many problems which perplex the human heart.   In the recognition of these problems, it is the office of Christian faith to trust the love of God."   Perhaps few modern believers ever rise to the stern devotion of Dante when he placed this inscription on the gates of Hell:

> Giustizia mosse il mio alto Fattore;
> Fecemi la divina Potestate,
> La somma Sapienza e il primo Amore.

"Justice it was that moved my high Maker; Divine Power made me, Supreme Wisdom, and Primal Love." Yet, as his commentator Witte has said, "Hell itself is neither more nor less than the protraction of unrepented sin, the symbolical interpretation of the sinful life." The torments are "but the sins themselves, revealed in their essence, recognized by their results; . . . the souls of the condemned have made their choice in this life, and work out their own damnation." The penalty of unrepented sin is to sin on; "he that is unrighteous, let him do unrighteousness still; he that is filthy, let him be even more filthy." Justice still reigns, and universal law; in Shakespeare's phrase, "We still have judgment here." Hell is not so much a place or state of vindictive retribution meted out by an angered Deity, in this conception—the highest Christian conception of the final woe—as a self-wrought infliction, inescapable in the nature of things, from which no amount of anguish can altogether free the soul.

The psychological origins of this doctrine lie deep. If too much has been made of it in the past, it may be true that the little which is made of it in the present only reflects the shallowness of our spiritual experience. For a deeply religious mind, the conception is full of meaning, and cannot be dealt with light-heartedly.   As the author of *Theologia Germanica* wrote, "This hell [the realization of what separation from God means to the soul] and this heaven [the desire of the eternal Good] are two good, safe ways for a man to travel in this present time, and happy is he who truly findeth them!"

II

Immortality in Modern Thought

It can scarcely be gainsaid that faith in immortality has not at the present time the hold upon men's minds which it formerly possessed. Many factors have combined to produce this situation, the more important of which will be considered in the present chapter. Down to and including the generation of our grandfathers, some form or other of belief in an after-life was undisputed by most men. And it may even be that an actual majority, possibly even a large majority at the present time, do not deny the survival of the soul beyond death. However, it is one of the significant contrasts between our century and the last—at least up to its middle decades—that immortality, even when not denied, has ceased to hold its place in men's thoughts, to influence their actions and mould their ideas of life in general as once it did. They are willing, perhaps, "to admit the great Beyond, and then leave it severely alone." Many share the feeling of Frederic Myers' host, who affirmed, "Of course, if you press me, I believe that we shall all enter into eternal bliss; but I wish you would not talk about such disagreeable subjects!" Or they belong to the class described by Sir William Osler as "the immense majority" who accept belief in immortality, and accept the phrases and forms of the prevailing religion, but live practically uninfluenced by it.

It is natural to ascribe this change of outlook to the development of modern scientific investigation and discovery: not only the positive facts about the universe which science has found out, but the whole attitude of scientific thought, especially its unwillingness to grant to an unproved hypothesis or a professed revelation the validity of ascertained and demonstrable fact. On the other hand, we may note an increasing interest in the question, not only among persons directly affected by the holocaust of the war, but also those naturally hungering for a more spiritual interpretation of life than can be satisfied either by purely scientific thought or by the widespread materialism which modern industry seems to encourage. For some, the phenomena of spiritualism are of chief interest and hold the greatest promise of satisfaction. Spiritualism—or, preferably, *spiritism*—is of course not modern but dates from earliest antiquity; but it has come forward in our day to offer just those demonstrations which the scientific attitude demands: tangible, or at least audible and visible, proofs of human survival. The popularity of this interest is attested by the theater, which in recent years, during the period between the two World Wars, has produced such arresting dramas as Sir James Barrie's *A Well-Remembered Voice*, Alice Gerstenberg's *Beyond*, John Balder-

ston's *Berkeley Square,* Sutton Vane's *Outward Bound,*
Walter Ferris' version of Alberto Casella's *Death Takes
a Holiday,* and Paul Osborn's *On Borrowed Time.*
For others, the way of escape from uncertainty and
agnosticism is a return to the orthodox Catholic doctrine with its practices, prayers for the dead, invocation
of saints, and the belief in Purgatory. Viewed sympathetically, we may see in this an effort, perhaps only
partly conscious, to revive the ethos of faith and to
realize once more in devotional life the "communion
of saints" which is still a formal article of belief in most
Christian churches. In still other circles, Theosophy
and the study of occult lore have seemed most full of
promise. Nor must the revival of Millennarianism
during recent years be overlooked, especially in the
United States, where it has produced at least a stiffening
of defense among conservatives who still maintain a
literal biblicism in their view of the future. The modern interest in mysticism is another indication pointing
in the same direction, namely, towards dissatisfaction
with the secular and scientific outlook upon life and a
widespread longing for news of that other world which
must contain the solution, if solution there is to be, of
the riddle of destiny and the enigma of our existence.

§

It is not necessary for one to be a professional student
of science to share the modern scientific view of the
world. Newspapers and magazines and popular books

have provided it with a far-reaching propaganda. Our poetry, our literature generally, our public education, even the pulpit is influenced by this attitude. Men of today realize the brevity of life, the universality of change, the instability and uncertain significance of social and individual life as never before. If it be true, as modern science assures us, that our race is only a newcomer upon a planet unimaginably old; that man is not the being for whose comfort or in whose interest the heavens and the earth were finished in six days, but only a fortuitous product of an evolutionary process which began several hundred million years ago—as Bergson has described him, only "Nature's latest experiment"; that our aged luminary, the parent sun of this planetary system, is relatively but a tiny speck of incandescent gas adrift in starry space; then the age-long question, "What is man?" can be answered only by confused silence. Let us cover our faces in shame and with Job refrain from boastful, unmeaning words! The question has but one answer, and man's dream of survival beyond death cannot be taken seriously.

Not only are the picturesque cosmologies of the elder poets, Dante and Milton, no longer tenable, but the religious view of man's origin and destiny which they expounded has become meaningless for many persons. The imagination no longer clothes Christian doctrine in the attractive forms and symbols of ancient speculation; imagination itself is overwhelmed by new and unforeseen but demonstrable facts! We are aware, in

Ludwig Lewisohn's phrase, of "our homelessness in the
universe, our terrible helplessness before it"; and of the
lack of any point of permanence in what William James
called "the vast driftings of the cosmic weather." Everything flows, and there is no point of finality anywhere
save the point of death; on the material side, even this
point is not final. This is no new sentiment; we only
formulate it in more scientific terms than those of early
Greek philosophy or Hebrew wisdom. The soul still
cries out for a Power with whom is no variableness,
neither shadow of turning, and apparently that cry is
in vain.

> Time goes, you say? Ah no!
> Alas, Time stays, *we* go.

The physical sciences have wrought this much of change
in man's view of his own nature, and hence of the pos-
sibilities of his future. The visible heavens no longer
"declare the glory of God"; instead, they oppress us with
a feeling of immensity, from which our own significance
has disappeared, and from which His presence seems
also to have vanished. And beyond the visible stars
and planets in our skies, revealed only to the searching
gaze of the astronomer,

> Out of keenest sight
> A myriad more pursue their pathless way
> Unerring, through the awful space, where day
> Is not, but an unending fearful night
> Shrouds the immensity. . . . The soul
> Of man should faint could he but see the whole!

Here upon earth the vast, substantial, everlasting hills likewise fade before the research of the geologist, who tells us that the heart of the North American continent has lain full fifteen times beneath the ocean floor!

> There rolls the deep where grew the tree.
>   O earth, what changes hast thou seen!
>   There where the long street roars hath been
> The stillness of the central sea.
>
> The hills are shadows, and they flow
>   From form to form, and nothing stands;
>   They melt like mist, the solid lands,
> Like clouds, they shape themselves and go.

What is man?   "Shall a creature so puny and frail," asks Sir J. G. Frazer, "claim to live for ever, to outlast not only the present starry system but every other that, when earth and sun and stars have crumbled into dust, shall be built on their ruins in the long hereafter?" The only answer that seems possible is Hume's: "If any principle of nature is clear, we may affirm that the whole scope and intention of man's creation, so far as we can judge by natural reason, is limited to this life." We are but creatures of a process whose meaning and full reach we cannot ascertain,

> And Whither vainer sounds than Whence
>   For word with such wayfarers.

Now it must certainly be recognized that *physical* science is not the whole of science; and also that the significance of any process is to be read neither in its beginnings nor its intermediate steps, but in its final culmination. The nearer we approach its culmination, the more accurately we shall be able to ascertain its meaning. As Meredith has elsewhere testified,

> Earth was not earth before her sons appeared;

and though the full "reading of earth" may teach man that Nature

> will soothe his need,
> Not his desire,

there may nevertheless be a stage in human development where need and desire are one, where the very rationality of existence demands permanence for those ends or values or persons whose evolution the whole interminable effort of nature has subserved. There may be more scientific and philosophic truth than we suspect in the statement of St. Paul that "the whole creation groaneth and travaileth in pain," waiting for "the revealing of the sons of God." Among modern scientists there are those who have expressed a view not wholly dissimilar to this. The words of Darwin are well known: "Believing as I do that man in the distant future will be a far more perfect creature than he now is, it is an intolerable thought that he and all other sentient beings are doomed to complete annihilation after such long-continued, slow progress." More positive is the statement of John Fiske: "The more thoroughly we comprehend that process of evolution by which things have come to be what they are, the more we are likely to feel that to deny the everlasting spiritual element in man is to rob the whole process of its meaning.   It goes far toward putting us to permanent intellectual confusion, and I do not see that any one has as yet alleged, or is ever likely to allege, a sufficient reason for our accepting so dire a conclusion."

The gravest defect in many arguments against immortality that are urged on the basis of natural science is a defect of imagination.   Physical science deals with a universe which thus far, so our scientists confess, passes human comprehension, whose processes can only in a very fragmentary and often hypothetical way be mapped out.   To identify the totality of existence, or the totality of value or truth, with what can be ascertained by test-tube or statistics, or weighed and measured by any scientific instrument or formula, is the height of folly.   In so doing, science would be cutting the ground from beneath its own feet and casting doubt upon the meaning and validity of its own inferences. If man is but the by-product of a course of evolution still in progress, a species fated sometime to become as extinct as *megatherium,* without preservation of any trace of his existence other than his fossil bones or some vestiges of that universal havoc which he has wrought among other species during his brief sojourn upon this planet, then what reason remains for supposing that the mind by which he searches out the hidden causes of things is more than the by-product of his hunger or ambition? He has chosen his facts; his inferences only reflect his desires. The "objective" world of science is then no more the real world than is the fanciful one of the mental invalid. Science requires firmer standing-ground than this.

§

If we turn now to the sciences which more closely affect the individual and his hope of immortality, namely, biology and psychology, we meet with a point of view which, if pressed to its logical conclusion, might require us to forego all hope of survival after death. Yet this point of view is not the only one to be found in contemporary thought in these fields; there is an alternative, and scientists themselves have pointed this out.

At the lowest levels, as at the highest, all living things seem to consist of a colloidal substance called proto-plasm. In the most elementary biological forms, this may be described in the words of Professor J. Y. Simp-son, as "viscid and translucent, generally colorless, im-miscible in water, and yet composed of it sometimes to the extent of ninety *per cent*. Chemically analyzed, after treatment by reagents, which rob it of its essential character, it is found to consist of carbon, oxygen, nitro-gen, hydrogen, and sulphur, together with traces of various salts." Its chief characteristics are the fact of its organization, its cellular structure and power of reproduction by cellular division, its incessant activity and response to stimulus, its ability to transform energy and maintain itself by growth.   But what confers these powers upon "animate" matter, as distinguished from "inanimate," science does not say.   "The mere fact," continues Professor Simpson, "that the first touch of the chemical reagent . . . robs it of its distinctive character shows that life is not material; we know life only in association with matter, yet it is not matter.   A cat weighs no more and no less after the loss of its proverbial nine lives than it did in life.   If life were material, then *ex hypothesi* it ought to weigh more in life than in death. . . . Life, then, is not matter, nor is it exhausted by the concept of matter.   In itself it occupies no space; it has no weight as we know gravity.   It may be figured as the flow of something—a procession."

Nor is life identical with energy; its function is rather the direction and control of energy.   Every living thing is a center for the transformation of energy—energy which may be accurately computed, in most cases—and a point of resistance to the natural tendency towards its degradation.   It is also, and this is far more significant, a "directive channel" along which energy can flow to accomplish certain specific work.   While the organism is alive, it continually disturbs the equilibrium which would otherwise be established between itself and its environment—an equilibrium which chemical change produces after death. It constantly selects, accumulates, directs this energy in life, and by reproduction passes on the ability to repeat the process. Thus neither the physico-chemical properties of matter, nor the concept of energy itself, yields us the clue to the nature of life or its powers of self-maintenance and reproduction. As Professor Edmund Wilson puts it, "We no more know how the organization of the germ cell involves the properties of the adult body than we know how the properties of hydrogen and oxygen involve those of water." The origin of life—and certainly it "originated," if once this planet was too hot to sustain any form of life which we now know or whose vestiges geology is able to trace—the origin of life is a subject of speculation for which, it must be admitted, science has scarcely any data. The hypothesis that it drifted hither through the cosmic spaces only removes by one step the essential problem of its origin. In the end we must assume, with Sir Oliver Lodge, that "life may be something not only ultra-terrestrial, but even immaterial, something outside our present categories of matter and energy; as real as they are, but different, and utilizing them for its own purpose."

If life is essentially immaterial, then it may be that its external manifestations in nature are really the expressions of some power or purpose more akin to those which we denominate "psychical," that it represents a teleology of will which were properly written with a capital. In the activities of even the humblest living creatures, we are driven to postulate an inner and purposive character whose results, rather than causes, are these activities. "An organism is never an automaton; it is a teleological unity whose simplest reactions have a purposive meaning" (Principal G. Galloway). For the student of philosophy and theology, it must be impressive to recall that Plotinus in one of his earliest expositions anticipated a view which modern science is leading us to assume. "It is absurd, or rather impossible," he says, "that life should be the product of an aggregation of bodies, or that things without understanding should generate mind."

The biological significance of death is not exactly definable. As Marcus Aurelius long ago wrote in his *Meditations,* "Death, like generation, is the secret of nature." Reproduction, and especially over-fertility, may be taken as nature's method of meeting the dangers incident to animate existence in an otherwise mechanistic universe—where life might conceivably be blotted out, as by alterations of climate, temperature, or geologic change. And over-fertility, if not reproduction itself, implies death. Death, as the sequel of reproduction, makes possible the development of species, and indeed the whole evolutionary process; and we may say that in general death has operated to the advantage of the whole universe of life. The precise "quantity" of animation, as in a vegetable seed, is ordinarily indeterminable save by actual experiment, by trying to make it grow; animation itself appears to be a quality. Whatever its ultimate nature, life is the manifestation of a quality whose absence is "death." In accordance with recent experiments there appear to be low forms of life which enjoy a natural or biological immortality. Dr. Alexis Carrel has demonstrated, with a bit of tissue from the heart of a chicken, that there is "no known limit to the ability of cells in a favorable environment to maintain life, health, and youth." The normal function of "death" in those larvae and moths which undergo cyclic transformations is well known; though even here it may be viewed as nature's effort to escape or to overcome the fatalities incident to organic, structural existence. "Everything," as Bergson said, "*is as if* this death had been willed, or at least accepted, for the greater progress of life in general."

§

Nor does man step outside this universal life when he develops the qualities of a moral and intellectual being, for man is "organic to nature" in all his works and ways. "The specific human experiences cannot be taken as an excrescence on the universe or as a self-contained and underived world by themselves. . . . The ethical predicates must carry us nearer to a true definition of the ultimate Life in which we live than the categories of environment" (A. S. Pringle-Pattison).

The specific point at which the question of immortality involves the science of psychology is the still-unsolved problem of the relation between mind and brain. Modern physiological study of the structure and processes of the human and animal brain has opened up a field of research by no means yet exhausted, though the investigations completed thus far have permanently shifted the science upon new foundations. It has been definitely shown that certain areas of the brain are the functional seats of the various ideo-motor processes affecting human thought and activity. "Organic selection has determined that the right side of the body should be 'served' by the left side of the brain—perhaps because a right limb is more frequently exercised than a left, while the blood is more rapidly and effectively circulated through the left hemisphere, as Wundt suggests. The right *limb* requires more frequent renewal of its material, which the left *brain* is more able to supply. Hence functions which are not bilaterally developed, such as those involved in speech, the appreciation and production of music, and mathematical calculation, are also relegated to the left side of the brain" (Professor J. L. McIntyre). At the same time, variations from this rule occur, as in left-handedness, or as the result of injury followed by re-learning through the compensation or vicarious functioning of the opposite hemisphere. Nor is the normal functioning of particular areas an absolute rule. Primitively, the allotment of areas is a matter of indifference, and nothing in the nature of things forbids the visual area, for example, to function in the service of the auditive consciousness. In certain cases of injury new areas may be employed, adjacent to the one destroyed.

From the existence of such phenomena, one might perhaps draw the conclusion that mind is only the product of brain, as the liver secretes bile or a boiling pot sends out steam. Or it may be concluded that brain and mind are parallel in their functions, never really reacting the one upon the other. The former inference is no longer supported by any considerable authority, though it enjoyed prestige for a time in the nineteenth century under the guise of "epiphenomenalism." Modern physiology has done away with the "secretion" theory of mind, since it has made clear that "form is a manifestation of function, and the essence of life is activity, not organization" (E. S. Russell, in *Form and Function*). It would in truth be more correct to say, on the basis of this probability, that "brain" is the secretion of "mind"! Moreover, the theory usually known as "parallelism" may now be said to be practically abandoned in favor of "interaction," namely, that mind and brain though nominally independent do react upon each other. What a man thinks and feels affects the centers of the brain, and indeed his whole nervous system; on the other hand, the condition of these centers and of the body generally, as in rest or fatigue, health or disease, affects his thinking and feeling. In a word, the theory of interaction is little more than descriptive of a situation that everyone recognizes. The question, Which is primary, mind or brain? is scarcely answered by these inferences or descriptive hypotheses. It would seem, however, that certain facts point in the direction of the primacy of mind, though this primacy is constantly conditioned by the twin factors of opportunity and use. "The mind itself and the environment determine between them the structure of their intermediary, the brain." It is as a living whole, body, nerves, brain, and mind, that man enjoys consciousness. And in this unity the mind, through the feelings and will, is dynamic and exercises a superior control. Not only, that is, among these various factors, is the mind *primus inter pares;* there are also indications that the mind—not limiting it, of course, to the conscious mind—exercises a still higher office. For example, small as it is in size, the human brain is much larger than man in his present state of development requires. The mind has thus far made use of only a certain section of it. There are areas of which no demonstrable use is made, though the part used increases in extent as civilization advances. The same is true of the individual—where the increase takes place, for example, in the learning of new languages. And though Klaatsch has shown that the other primates were prevented from developing speech through physiological inadaptibility, on account of the size and location of facial muscles and the form of the mouth, it does not necessarily follow that human speech is purely accidental. Man evidently tried to speak, had a desire for speech, before expressive sounds were produced. We find here a significant confirmation of William James' assertion that the phenomena of consciousness "may imply not the production but the transmission of mind by brain." As he stated his conviction in a letter to Bergson, "the brain is an organ of *filtration* for spiritual life!" From this Kant's speculative inference is surely legitimate, "The death of the body may indeed be the end of the sensational use of our mind, but only the beginning of its intellectual use. The body would thus be not the cause of our thinking, but merely a condition restrictive thereof; and, although essential to our sensuous and animal consciousness, it may be regarded as an impeder of our purely spiritual life."

It is surely reasonable, therefore, to hold that the mind, even though we may not go so far as to claim for it priority in time—or preëxistence—but only primacy among the factors that make up man's conscious existence, may quite possibly survive the breakdown of the body and brain. That the mind dies with the brain is pure assumption, for which we possess no justifying data whatsoever. Restorations of memory following states of amnesia caused by physical lesion or concussion point to an at least temporary survival or inde-

pendence of the mind. Thus we may claim a certain
probability of the mind's survival, even while recognizing the lowly beginnings of human consciousness both
in the individual and in the race. The position of
T. H. Green is assuredly not disconsonant with modern
scientific psychology: "In the growth of our experience,
an animal organism which has its history in time gradually becomes the vehicle of an eternally complete
consciousness. What we call our mental history is not
a history of this consciousness, which in itself can have
no history, but a history of the process by which the
animal organism becomes its vehicle."

That such a view harmonizes with the religious belief in immortality may be shown by reference to Origen, who used of course the language of his day and not
modern psychological terminology: "It is out of the
animal body that the very power and grace of the resurrection educe the spiritual body, when it transmutes it
from a condition of indignity to one of glory." Origen's doctrine need not be taken to imply the now-
discarded theory of "soul-substance." As Professor Galloway says, it is "the experience of the self as a *spiritual*
substance or reality unifying its changing states which is
the source whence we derive that notion of substance
as the supposed ground of qualities in the external
world." In a word, science itself is still animistic! No
one thinks the soul is merely a "harmony" of the bodily
elements, as Plato's opponents held. It is simple, and

no *syntheton*. It is something deeper, the predisposing condition or cause of that "harmony." Let us, however, use the word *self*, rather than "soul," and understand by it no more than that mysterious something, x, which makes possible the unity of conscious life and insures its continuity. The self may be, and probably is, something more than a function of brain, as it certainly is more than a material "stuff" or quasi-material "force." If so, then why should we not suppose that this "self" triumphs over death as it does over other if lesser obstacles to its persistence, such as sleep, injuries, or loss of memory?—or as when "some infernality of the body prevents really existing parts of the mind from coming to their effective rights at all, suppresses them, and blots them out from participation in this world's experiences" (William James, Letter to his sister, July 6, 1891).

On such a view, the old question, At what point of development did the individual become or "receive" a soul? is meaningless. Neither the traducianism or the creationism of ancient theology, nor any theory of modern psychology, satisfactorily answers it. The *individual* always was a "soul": in the instant, whether or not that instant is determinable, when he became an individual, he became a potential "self"; and all the experience and the growth of years have been but the process of the development of this self. It is not "received" at a point in time. Its growth is a process spread over months and years and decades; and, we may add, there is apparently no reason to suppose that it may not continue after death, unless progress be conceived in terms entirely conditioned upon an existence within time and space. The question is sometimes asked in another form: At what point in human evolution did man begin to be capable of immortality? For example, were the men of the Old Stone Age immortal, or the earliest examples of the human species, as distinct from other primates? But the question is really unanswerable. The terms and the conceptions which it involves are really self-contradictory. In strict truth, it was not *as men*, or as members of a species of higher primates, that they were or that we are potentially immortal. The true question, rather, is, At what point does man become a *self*? To this question neither science nor theology nor common sense has a sufficient answer. Our experience has not been gained in palaeolithic times, nor do our individual memories reach far enough back. The same difficulty attaches to the question concerning the immortality of the lower animals, for example of dogs, who sometimes manifest intelligence and "virtue," such as loyalty, honesty and affection, and whose immortality is assumed not only by primitive men but by some modern writers. Philosophically, the question becomes, Has—or is—the lower animal a "self"?

Nor is such existence or persistence of the "self" de-

pendent upon the retention of memory. It is enough
if consciousness of identity survives. Even in this life,
completely conscious memory is not essential to continuity of consciousness. The content of our memory
—and in this degree the identity of the "self"—is always
changing. We forget many things, and we remember
others. We "recollect" events, circumstances, experiences, facts, long forgotten. Parts of our past may disappear, temporarily at least, though some psychologists
maintain that nothing is ever really "forgotten," but
every memory is filed away in the subconscious mind.
To be told of certain of our experiences is sometimes
like being told of the experience of another person.
The problem of memory is therefore secondary and
incidental to the survival of the self. There are philosophers, like McTaggart, who hold that even without
conscious memory survival of the self is both possible
and desirable. And although Aristotle for this reason
denied that the blest could be happy, Dante does not
hesitate to represent his own experience, a foretaste of
that of the beatified saints in Paradise, as contentment
with such a state:

> For that, so near approaching its desire,
> Our intellect is to such depth absorb'd,
> That memory cannot follow.

The earthly experience upon which this conception is
based is doubtless that of spiritual exaltation and ecstasy.

In view of the facts that have been adduced, and of

the legitimate inferences that have been drawn from them, no counting of heads, such as Dr. Leuba undertook in his questionnaire addressed to five-hundred scientists and students, or the American Branch of the Society for Psychical Research with its more than three-thousand replies, is of any decisive value. It is a problem which each man must solve for himself; and no reference to authorities, *pro* or *contra,* can possibly mean more to him than an appeal to other men's beliefs in preference to his own. Nor may a much more favorable judgment be passed upon the results of modern psychical investigation. Even the most positive of them scarcely warrant a belief in immortality; they imply little more than a limited survival of the soul after death (and do not imply even this very certainly), and usually under conditions that are either simply appalling or reflect too completely conditions which we might well hope to leave behind at death. Often, too, they reflect only the heartfelt yearnings of the earthly survivors. One need not rule out the possibility of communication with the departed; one may even go so far as to hold, with Frederic Myers, that the revival of psychic phenomena in recent times points to a strong and repeated effort "from the other side" to bridge the gulf and assure us that all is well. Yet the successive unmaskings of pretended mediums, and the uncertainty whether or not, after all, even the fullest "demonstrations" are not explainable upon the hypothesis of telepa-

thy or mind-reading, must incline us to feel, with Leslie
Stephen, that "the majestic doubt of our natural hope of
immortality" is more trustworthy than "these ghostly
voices." The search for tangible and indisputable evidence,

> unfaith clamouring to be coined
> To faith by proof,

is itself unrecognized evidence of the deep longing in
men's hearts for the thing itself. But it usually has the
result, ethically and religiously, of binding us still more
firmly to earthly conditions. Such faith as a rule, if
faith it be, is not content to move within the sphere of
probability; it stakes its all upon scientific demonstration. And if this fails, it too must yield, for it has no
further appeal.

> Strange, is it not?—that of the myriads who
> Before us passed the door of darkness through
> Not one returns to tell us of the road
> Which to discover we must travel too.

Omar's problem is one which men in every age have
felt, save those who believed the longing for positive
demonstration to have been answered. On the other
hand, almost everyone who has believed in immortality
has agreed with Martineau: "We do not believe in immortality because we can prove it; we try to prove it
because we cannot help believing it." And though, for
the Christian, the resurrection of Christ is the answer

to this perennial questioning, it must be acknowledged that what Christ's resurrection has given us is, primarily, the assurance of his victory over death, not a descriptive statement of conditions in the life beyond.

§

"The universe is change," wrote the emperor Marcus Aurelius, "and our life is what our thoughts make it." At the least, however, modern science has assured us of the universality of order, despite and throughout all change. Even chaos has its laws, if we may identify that state described by poets and philosophers with what we today observe in distant nebular whorls and luminous blots upon the starry heavens. So has it been, ever since the dawn of the physical creation.

> Around the ancient track marched, rank on rank,
> The army of unalterable law.

As Münsterberg wrote, in a classic description of Naturalism, "Necessity moves the stars in the sky, and necessity moves the emotions of my mind"; or, in Huxley's words, "As for the strong conviction that the cosmic order is rational, and the faith that, throughout all durations, unbroken order has reigned in the universe, I not only accept it, but I am disposed to think it the most important of all truths." And man, who is far from being a creature finished and final, but "still in process of creating himself," is also under the dominion of this cosmic order. We may well be thankful that this is so.

For it would be an intolerable situation if at any moment caprice might enter the universe, and either terminate at once or irresistibly deflect not only the process of our own development but the whole course of nature's ceaseless striving. We may all trust, with the scientist, that this is not so, and never will be so. Ours may in truth be no more than "the best of possible universes," neither yet, nor ever, so far as we can foresee, destined to become perfect in every particular—whatever that might be. We may likewise trust that the future of the world will be better than its past, that "the best is yet to be" for the whole race as for ourselves as individuals. As G. Stanley Hall expressed it, "Man as he exists today is only the beginning of what he is to be, the pygmoid or embryo of his true self"—endowed, perhaps, with other and higher senses than the five he now possesses. Nevertheless, it is quite improbable that science yields us the *whole* truth of life, a suspicion which man's immaturity in the present and the history of science in the past alike support. For this reason, the last word upon immortality may not be that of science, or of science as interpreted by unbelief, and Bertrand Russell's *Free Man's Worship* not our only possible creed. "Only within the scaffolding of these truths," he says, "only on the foundation of unyielding despair, can the soul's habitation henceforth be safely built!" For after all, it cannot be too often affirmed, the natural sciences deal only with a selected world of experience, and deal with it, as Principal Galloway said, at "a level on which the principles that only can decide the issue do not come under review." Science "works," like a mathematical solution, within its own limitations; "but the limits are narrow; and the human spirit experiences or divines much that extends beyond them." It may well remain, as Dean Inge has declared, "the constructive task which lies before the next century . . . to spiritualize science, as morality and art have already been spiritualized." The world is waiting for a spiritual philosophy which will take account of science, recognizing its validity within its own sphere, but keeping it in its proper place, and supplying that frame or foundation of thought without which science itself cannot make its full contribution to our understanding of the universe. Already we note signs that science has renounced materialism. Long ago Huxley remarked, "If the belief in immortality is essential to morality, physical science has no more to say against the probability of that doctrine than the most ordinary experience has, and it effectually closes the mouths of those who pretend to refute it by objections deduced from merely physical data." More recently, Professor McTaggart has thrown down a challenge to materialism which that philosophy, once proclaiming itself the only valid philosophy of science, can hardly answer: "If a man is shut up in a house, the transparency of the windows is an essential condition of his seeing the sky. But it would not be prudent to infer that if he walked out of the house he could not see the sky, because there was no longer any glass through which he might see it."

Man has rights which nature may ignore, but which cannot be ignored in the end—though in speaking of "nature" we of course only personify the complex of energy and law which produce the physical universe. It may be that this anthropomorphic "nature" has not the least intention of ignoring or slighting man! And it may even be true, granting all that science has discovered about the world in which we belong, that man and his destiny have all along been contemplated as an important and integral part of nature's process; and that, conversely, nature supplies and ministers to an important part of man's evolution and destiny; that nature, the physical universe, the complex of energy and law, is only one phase of a vast and essentially spiritual process in which man has a vital and inalienable share. "The universe shows us two aspects," says Professor Whitehead: "on one side it is physically wasting, on the other side it is spiritually ascending. It is thus passing with a slowness, inconceivable in our measures of time, to new creative conditions, amid which the physical world, as we at present know it, will be represented by a ripple barely to be distinguished from non-entity." Such a flowering of the universe in some higher and hitherto unsuspected state of existence is an open possibility from the point of view of physics;

for religion, however, something more is required, something that it is not mere egotism for the individual to
ask. We may call this the coming of the Kingdom of
God, or the eternal life of man, or the self-realization
of the Absolute, or what we will, using religious or meta-
physical terms; but it is certain that science, though it
may suggest a teleology sweeping all existence, animate
and inanimate, into its course, does not give us the final
secret, the goal and end towards which the strivings of
the universe unceasingly tend. In the words of the
early Christian writer, "It doth not yet appear what
we shall be."

Of course it may be questioned, and modern speculative physics does indeed raise the question, whether
the universe can ever really "disappear"—save in the
purely verbal sense of lacking a perceiving subject to
whom to appear. If we grant the doctrine that matter
is nothing more than various "forms of energy," and
also assume the principle of the degradation of energy—
at least in this part of the universe, within our own
decadent solar and planetary system (though the universe as a whole may, as Professor Eddington holds, be
'expanding')—what then will become of this energy
after it is once more reduced to formlessness? In other
words, what is to remain after this universal energy has
spent and exhausted itself? Such a question is one
more that is unanswerable, save, possibly, upon a purely
spiritual and purposive interpretation of nature: the

universal energy, lapsing again into its primal Fount, may then, conceivably, once more spring forth and produce another universe different in kind from that which we now see. Such lapse and renewal might even be conceived as gradual, constant, simultaneous processes, given an unlimited quantity of energy. Between the purely "spiritual" and the purely "material" there yawns an impassable gulf for much of modern thinking. Nevertheless, if only for the sake of unity and progress in thought, this gulf must somehow be bridged. The external universe can no more remain valueless for the human spirit than spirit remain without significance for the world of matter. Neoplatonism and early Christian mysticism, and in fact every philosophy save a hopelessly dualistic idealism, have found a way to bridge this gulf. As Milton suggests,

> What if earth
> Be but the shadow of heaven, and things therein
> Each to other like more than on earth is thought?

Monistic materialism alone ignores the existence of this gulf; but it is there, nevertheless.

§

Nature's ends, at least as far as we are able to define them at the present stage of evolution, are in some degree realized in man; but where and how are man's ends to be realized? This question, the immemorial query of philosophy, leads us out of the realm of science,

of physical phenomena, into that of metaphysics. That
is, it leads us into a larger field which still encloses the
smaller, like a park surrounding a garden. For modern
philosophy is largely concerned with the data of scientific research; one might even call it a metaphysics of
science. And not science only but all humane studies
are embraced like so many provinces within the wide
empire of philosophy. As Bosanquet said of social
morality, art, philosophy, and religion, they "take us
far beyond the spatio-temporal externality of history"
and of scientific research; yet they and science have not
ceased to be mutually related. Philosophy itself con-
ceives that the universe we know is only a part of a
larger and possibly infinite whole; it introduces us to a
sphere of values, of intellectual and moral realities transcending all that can be "touched and tasted and han-
dled" or dealt with after any external fashion. Yet we
find these values inextricably associated with the world
of things. It is not "another" world; the two spheres
interpenetrate, though they are not necessarily homo-
centric or homogeneous for modern philosophy. "We
cannot believe that anything in life is meaningless, or
has no significance beyond the fleeting moment." This
provides the starting-point for philosophy, since the
meaning of things is, more often than not, deeply and
mysteriously shrouded from the peering gaze of physical research. Moreover, as Lotze pointed out, "the
finite being does not contain in itself the conditions of

its own existence," and by implication, therefore, pre-supposes a vaster whole of which it is a part, which guarantees both its existence and its meaning.

This elementary principle of any intelligent consideration of the phenomenon of knowledge has made a wide appeal to modern thought. "Nothing can come out of nothing," as the Stoical emperor affirmed, "any more than a thing can go back to nothing." More recently, we have the assumption by Professor Pringle-Pattison—still upon Stoical lines—of a *rerum natura* to which nothing can be added; development implies previous existence in the nature of things. Here is the beginning, perhaps, of a new "phenomenology," a new and yet essentially old interpretation of the facts of life, existence, knowledge, as outward and visible signs of inward and invisible realities whose partial manifestation they are, and which contain the secret of their significance. There is also to be found in recent thought a notable trend in the direction of symbolism and mysticism. As Dean Inge has defined it, mysticism views the real world as created by the thought and will of God, and existing in His mind. "It is therefore spiritual, and above space and time, which are only the forms under which reality is set out as a process." The ultimate identity of existence and value is "the venture of faith to which mysticism and speculative idealism are committed." As Plotinus said, "The soul is immaterial and immortal, for it belongs to the world of real existence, and nothing that *is* can cease to be. . . . The body is in the soul, rather than the soul in the body." And as Inge has expounded this principle and its bearing upon the subject of our inquiry, in his Gifford Lectures on *The Philosophy of Plotinus,* "The religious faith in immortality is the faith that all true values are valid always and everywhere; that the order of the universe is just, rational and beautiful; and that those principles which exalt us above ourselves are the attributes of the Creator in whom we live and move and have our being."

Not only existence, then—which is of course a value, for the majority of human beings as for the ontological philosophers—but higher values as well must be guaranteed by some superior, encompassing Reality. Foremost among these is personality. If, as Browning held, "little else is worth study save the development of a soul," a conviction which the whole world of modern letters and philosophy would echo, then surely the human personality must have some ground, some *raison d'être,* beyond the bare satisfaction of the wants or service of the necessities of mortal existence. This was the testimony of Goethe, in his famous letter to Eckermann: "When a man is as old as I am, he is bound occasionally to think about death. In my case this thought leaves me in perfect peace, for I have a firm conviction that our spirit is a being indestructible by nature. It works on from eternity to eternity; it is like a sun which only seems to set, but in truth never sets but shines on unceasingly." It is "the paradox of our being: if death be death, life is not life; if life be life, death is not death" (G. Lowes Dickinson). If personality is the goal of our past evolution and of our present education and discipline, then eternal life surely cannot be anything less than that which personality itself demands, its full fruition and attainment in a conscious existence in God. "We base this claim on the soul's manifest transcendence, on its genuine reality, and on the general law of the persistence of real existence. . . . Immortality is the persistence of the essential and the real; it applies to things which the universe has gained— things which, once acquired, cannot be let go."

It is true, a considerable school of modern philosophy views this attainment of personality as an absorption or merging of our separate, individual consciousness in the "Absolute." This is a conception difficult to grasp, especially when we are told that it means no loss of the personal "self," as when Bosanquet defines "the eternal reality of the Absolute" as "that *realization* of our self which we instinctively demand and desire." In view of the history of this idea, one cannot say off-hand that it lacks religious value, or that upon such a hypothesis immortality ceases to be desirable, certainly not as Bosanquet has presented it. The history of Hindu religious thought, for example, is an insuperable obstacle to such a denial. Man's deliverance from out the bourne of time and place, of relativity and succession, of finite limitations, is for many religious minds a hoped-for deliverance from the burden of successive lives—even though this succession be itself a kind of immortality, overshadowed however by the notion of duration in a time-process. This deliverance takes place through knowledge, the saving knowledge that the soul is one with Brahma. In its light, "the illusion of individuality fades away, and the spirit reaches the haven of rest and peace." Otherwise conceived, as in Buddhism, the goal is reached with the extinction of all desire, even the desire for a future life. This passionless, undisturbed cessation of all striving is Nirvana—which is not a state of "nothingness," but, as in Christian mysticism, a state definable only in negative terms. No words can really describe it: hence the inability of most Occidentals to conceive it. Mystical experience alone gives content to the idea. Man goes

> Unto Nirvana. He is one with life,
> Yet lives not. He is blest, ceasing to be.
> *Om, Mani padme om!* the dewdrop slips
>   Into the shining sea.

Similar ideas, as we have said, are not unknown in western and Christian thought.

> To God again the enfranchised soul must tend;
> He is her home, her Author is her end;
> No death is hers; when earthly eyes grow dim,
> Starlike she soars and Godlike *melts in Him.*

As conceived by modern idealist philosophers of this school, for example by Dr. Bosanquet, the Absolute is the end and goal of all existence; nothing at last can escape absorption in the All. For this reason he insists that the human self, in spite of its sense of freedom, is not only destined finally for that goal but is even here and now an element in the Absolute. It is therefore "an inconceivable abstraction" to place eternity and perfection "in a future beyond time." This doctrine represents a denial upon philosophic grounds of the traditional or popular Christian view of immortality simply as a *future* state, a denial which, fortunately or unfortunately, is likely to take place whenever the conception of time and its relation to eternity is subjected to critical examination. For the moment, however, we may pause to inquire what it is that persists—or exists in the "eternal now" within the Absolute—to give value to life and provide man with a goal of personal moral and spiritual effort. How may values be conserved apart from personal lives which make these values real? As Professor Galloway points out, it is surely "an inconceivable abstraction" to speak of impersonal values! Or if "qualities persist, not quantities," how can a quality persist which is not a quality of something? Pure "quality" is a refinement of metaphysics, a term of thought and nothing more, like a scholastic "accident." And if my self is to be absorbed in another Self in such a way that I lose all identity and consciousness, what "value" can possibly remain, at least for me, in such an identification? If the Christian teaching be that "in God we live and move and have our being," it is still *we* who live and move. As Martineau asked, "Who can believe that the everlasting Mind fulfils its end by disappointing every other? . . . Is the eternal design of Perfection to be gained by the frustrated aspirations of countless ephemeral generations?" It may be said that the whole theory requires for its interpretation a transcendental experience; it is not a logical inference or an induction based upon external facts so much as an attempt to translate an ineffable spiritual experience into language which shall be reasonable and convincing—an experience which probably lies at the historical root of all philosophical idealism. "Absorption" is best understood, no doubt, by the analogy of human love: one self is "absorbed" in another, but not extinguished— like the ineffable love which glowed in the heavenly spheres of Dante's Paradise. Earthly love is the key to our realization of the heavenly. As Lowes Dickinson put it, this is "to be included in a larger self without losing one's own self, so that one could say, 'I am somehow that self.'" And even though this doctrine be rather too ambrosial for ordinary human nature's daily fare, its acceptance in certain high Christian circles, particularly in the Middle Ages, proves it to be not altogether disconsonant with our religion.

§

Graver still, perhaps, is the problem of time and its relation to eternity, as conceived not only by philosophy but also in the highest religious experience. What solution of the problem does philosophy offer us? And in what way does this solution affect our ordinary conception of immortality? For the ordinary, unphilosophical person, eternity is synonymous with endless duration. Time is duration which may be measured, and must therefore at some date or other come to an end: after which date eternity begins as duration without measure or end. In this view, eternity is an abstraction, though rendered as concrete and quantitative to the imagination as the terms allow. It has a recognizable value, for most men desire both to live and to live long; only the unhappy Brobdingnagians, weary of superfluous years in the midst of unchanging outward surroundings, grow restive with their fate. For this reason, in the ordinary conception, other conditions are required, in the midst of which men shall never grow weary.

If we seek the origin of this conception of eternity as endless perduration, we must go back once more to a spiritual experience. One of the deep roots of the early idealistic philosophy, even earlier than Plato and his school, is to be found in the cults of Orpheus and Dionysos in sixth and fifth century Hellas. In those religions, it seems probable, men of the West first became conscious, through religious ecstasy, of the soul's independence of the body. The soul, they found, was the real self—not just the body's shadow as primitive and Homeric religion had taught. And from this conception they came, still under the inspiration of ecstasy, to the belief that the soul, the real self, lives beyond the grave. "The mystic union of the soul with the god was the witness of its divine powers and its immortal nature" (Prin. Galloway). Thus a sense of timelessness, of elevation above the limitations and uncertainties of this present life, was introduced into Greek religion. Here was something that guaranteed to man that he himself should survive though the outward body fell into decay. From this point, it was an easy step to the idea of eternity beyond time, an idea which the classical philosophy of Greece took for granted, and to which it added the speculative conception (a logical implication of the idea itself) of duration backwards as well as forwards, of an everlasting state, without beginning or end. Some such process as this, no doubt, takes place in the mental development of all idealists and in the religious development of many Christians. The conclusion to which it leads, in the thought of immortality, seems more germane to Western ways of thinking than the original Semitic and Persian idea of a future resurrection. Our natural yearning is that of Browning:

> make time break
> And let us pent-up creatures through
> Into eternity, our due.

Emerson once replied to a fanatic who announced that the end of the world was approaching, "Very well; I can get along without it." Somehow, though perhaps inexplicably, eternity and time, the Infinite and the finite world, are not mutual contradictions; nor is the one but the prolongation of the other. The greater includes the less, and the passage from the finite to the Infinite is not extinction but release—out of the "prison-house," as Plato and the Orphic mystagogues expressed it, into the freedom of a larger life.

What then is time, viewed from this transcendental vantage-point of spiritual experience and philosophy? Has time any necessary part in our conception of "eternal life"? Eternal life and the temporal survival of death by the soul are of course not one and the same, though they may be taken as different descriptions of the same fact, from opposite points of view; yet the two must somehow be related to each other; and so must eternity and time. The schoolmen solved the riddle in a verbal way, by intercalating a medial state of duration, *aevum,* between time and eternity, partaking of some of the qualities of each. This they were in truth required to do by the ecclesiastical conception of the Intermediate State. But if modern science and philosophy permit us still to believe in immortality, it cannot be as mere survival, translation to another sphere essentially like this one, or projection of the personality into another time-series beyond the present; they require us to conceive, rather, of a translation to *another mode of existence*, outside the succession of nature. If one may hazard a definition of time, as involved in the modern scientific view of the universe, it is our measure of the slowing-down of energy, due to the hindrance of matter (itself a "form" of energy, as Bergson and modern electro-chemists agree in viewing it)—energy which would otherwise be instantaneous in its transformation. Time accordingly presupposes space and matter; and, upon this definition, time is "real." If the principle underlying the definition be true, then it is obvious that time itself must change in the course of certain millennia, as the solar system, for example, slows down, and energy is dissipated or degraded and no longer conserved. In a word, time though real is only relative, not absolute; and "mathematical" time is only an abstraction. It has often been pointed out that even in "mathematical" time, which is "pauseless flow," the mathematical *instant* has itself no duration, just as the geometrical point lacks extension. Accordingly, in Pringle-Pattison's words, "To think of time as a process is, *ipso facto,* to think of a reality which transcends time, and whose nature is revealed in the process." "If we were really subject to time, incapable of transcending it, we should be imprisoned each of us as a single point of particularity in its own moment of time. We should be absolutely unchanging because we should be reduced to the abstraction of a bare point of existence."

However, it is difficult to see how persons living within the time-process can think or speak in any other terms—recognizing of course that the "future" life is not limited to the future; that eternity does not "begin" at some future date, or eternal life exist only "after" this one. For in truth, relatively to our present, that life *is* future. Its realization comes at the end, or beyond the end, of this present course. We say that Chicago is west of New York, in terms of terrestrial longitude; whereas, in the great universe, through whose vast spaces swim and plunge our tiny globe and its fellow-planets, there is no East and West. It is only relatively to us that East and West have meaning, or past and future. It is only because the most impressive approach to that transcendent life is beyond the term of this one that we speak—and must speak—of it as "future." The "future life" is accordingly a true and useful term only in the sense of an imagined projection, beyond the time-series, of the process of living. In reality, as the highest philosophy and the intuitions of mysticism agree in representing it, the time-series will have ceased for us when that "future" becomes "present," and there shall then be no past or future but only an eternal now. Eternal life is still a future boon to us in our present course, save as exalted spiritual experience makes it a present reality and gives us a foretaste of its bliss; but time and all the affairs of time will neither cease to exist in fact nor lie buried in the "past," upon our entrance into eternity. They will be simply present, and simultaneous, in so far as they are real at all; if not present, then because not real, since "nothing that really is can ever cease to be." Only the process, the outward, causal succession will have disappeared, or will have ceased to involve us as one of its units. The mode of this presence of the past is doubtless akin to the presence of the past in memory. Released from succession, however, there seems no reason why the mind should not entertain the consciousness of realities directly and not their photographic images filed in the archives of memory.

Why then is time necessary at all? As religion and philosophy both view it, time is a necessary "condition of the exercise of the soul's capacities"; it is the school of the human spirit, the field of its discipline, its preparation or probation, its realization of God. Time is thus embraced within eternity, as one particular reality within the universal and supremely real, somewhat as our circling systems of stars and suns float or drift within the apparently endless spaces of the universe—the suns and stars whose motions in fact, together with the motion of the earth, provide our standard of measurement of time. But "beyond" space and "after" time, there is the Infinite and Eternal, embracing all. And to this Infinite and Eternal we are allied by the deepest, most secret yearnings of our nature, not to time and space, which provide only the conditions of our finite development.   The very fact that we are able to apprehend this truth that something lies above or beyond time and space would seem to imply what ancient thinkers called our "kinship with the divine," our natural affinity with the One, the Real, who is above and beyond all time. Our higher life, our very spiritual existence, like our thought, is thus a "flight" to the Transcendent and Eternal.

The conception of time is therefore inevitable, while we continue to exist as sharers in its process.   We cannot speak or think outside this category, though sometimes, perhaps, we can dimly feel.   We are its creatures, and cannot comprehend what lies "beyond" or "outside."   To the end, our thinking must be done in its terms.   For us, as for Plato, it is "the moving image of eternity"; and what we know or conceive of eternity is conditioned by our conception of time.   As Pringle-Pattison has truly said, "It is only through the characteristic features of time, through some transformation of these features, that we can form any intelligent conception of the eternal."   Nevertheless, though we must recognize the limitations that our present existence thus imposes upon us, limitations as inescapable for imagination and reflection as for our outward bodies, we know that the Real is beyond and above all time and place, unlimited, unhampered, unconfined.   And it is for a genuine deliverance from these our limitations that we deeply yearn; no doctrine of repeated cycles of ex-

istence within the time-process can satisfy our profoundest longings. The very notion contradicts our idea of
the self—largely determined as it is by heredity, on the
one hand, and on the other by the experiences and surroundings that we have known in this life; and it appears to us little better than the primitive belief whence
it springs, in which the soul is not the self and the survival of the soul implies no survival of personality.
What we require is, rather, an immortality that shall
transcend the power of time and change and circumstance: nothing less than initiation into the ultimate
Reality beyond all space and all time.

§

It is this sense of the limitations imposed upon us by
our finitude and dependence upon time and change
which makes possible the strongest appeal of the idea of
immortality to our generation. It is the old "moral
argument," not very much altered, but only stated in
another form: not the reversal of earth's injustices so
much as the success of man's moral efforts, the realization of his highest aims. For man, the present life is
inadequate. As James declared, giving his reason for
belief in personal immortality, he was "just getting fit
to live." No one fully attains his ideal in this world.
Even the best and most fortunate of us do not achieve
the good of which we feel capable and short of which we
cannot rest. The capacities of the soul are unexhausted

by the struggle. "The thing that at bottom matters most," as Lowes Dickinson put it in famous words, "is the sense of something in me making for more life and better. All my pain is at last a feeling of frustration of this; all my happiness a feeling of its satisfaction. I do not know what this is; I am not prepared to give a coherent account of it; I ought not, very likely, to call it 'it,' and to imply the category of substance. I will abandon, if necessary, under criticism, any particular terms in which I may try to describe it; I will abandon anything except itself. For it is real. It governs all my experience, and determines all my judgments of value." No one, not in the grip of intolerable evil, fails to sense this "urge" within him; it is a basic part of his nature; it is, in the language of theology and of Neoplatonic philosophy, the divine likeness within us tending upward to its original. And unless this spiritual instinct shall somehow be satisfied, our life here is doomed to hopeless frustration and incompleteness. This sublime faith was voiced by Professor Palmer when he wrote of his wife's death, "Though no regrets are proper for the manner of her death, who can contemplate the fact of it and not call the world irrational, if out of deference to a few particles of disordered matter it excludes so fair a spirit?" If death has any meaning other than the blank frustration and doom of all human hopes and purposes, it must be only a gateway unto larger life. As Royce held, "If death is real at all, it is real only in so far as it fulfils a purpose. But now, what purpose can be fulfilled by the ending of a life that is so far unfulfilled?" And to this testimony of faith Professor Ward has added, "In fine, the problem of evil seems insoluble, and any theodicy impossible, if this life be all."

The strongest argument for immortality is not logical, but personal: it is a noble life. Plato's arguments in the dialogue *Phaedo* are not altogether convincing; the real argument which convinced him and convinces us is the character of Socrates. "I had a singular feeling," he makes Phaedo say, "at being in his presence. I could hardly believe that I was present at the death of a friend, and therefore I did not pity him, Echecrates; his mien and his language were so noble and fearless in the hour of death that to me he appeared blessed. I thought that in going to the other world he could not be without a divine call, and that he would be happy, if any man ever was, when he arrived there." In fine, what convinced Plato was not an intellectual process but a moral experience, the association with his master; and his arguments are after all only "suggestive thoughts thrown out by a great mind which is striving to find a justification in the nature of things for a profound ethical faith." The heart really does have reasons that the reason can only ponder and formulate. Feeling is older, and deeper, in human nature than intellect, as the heart is biologically older than the brain; and it is the moral and religious experience underlying or preceding philosophy which is more convincing than any "proofs."

> What is excellent,
> As God lives, is permanent;
> Hearts are dust, hearts' loves remain;
> Heart's love will meet thee again.

As Richard Rothe said, in his *Stille Stunden,* "Whoever believes in God must also believe in the continuance of men after death"—not just as a logical inference from a spiritual existence, or from the justice or goodness of God, but as the most primary and fundamental implication of faith. It is this sense that we ourselves, and others, must "carry on" in a higher, better life which has inspired heroic souls as they stood on the shining ramparts for a moment and then sallied forth to keep their "rendezvous with Death." For them, "Death does not count," as Lewis Nettleship said. In a letter to his mother written shortly before he died, Alan Seeger voiced a conviction which less articulate thousands of his fellows shared: "Death is nothing terrible after all. It may mean something more wonderful than life. It cannot possibly mean anything worse to the good soldier."

All the same, these hours of vision or of intuition are not the whole of our lives, not even for those, our noblest and our best, who write their faith in action and immortalize their creeds in deeds of self-forgetting sacrifice. For some of us, life is very terrible and tragic; injustice and cruelty seem always to triumph over goodness and right. We must not dismiss too curtly the ancient argument, or conviction, that the injustices of this life must be wiped out and compensated in another. The weakness of the argument is obvious: it appears to offer a reward for suffering, and to appeal rather too strongly to men's natural self-interest. "Be good, and you will be happy—hereafter!" Its expression in the eudaemonism of certain religions, or, indeed, in one or another phase of almost all religions; its promise of Utopia in the next world, with the unsatisfied ambitions of this life guaranteed future satisfaction; its impotence to rouse men to heroic action in ending the evils of this world, content with looking forward to a divine interposition which shall right all wrong; its encouragement of a negative rather than a positive social attitude—all this is undeniable. Nevertheless, such criticism comes as a rule from those who are comfortably out of reach of tyranny and oppression, and who live in a world of philosophic calm or at least of political security. Men caught inescapably in a world where political freedom is a hopeless dream, or for whom death alone can bring release from constant pain or overwhelming grief, do not feel the force of these criticisms. The world as they know it is far from perfect, and they

cannot believe it perfect in the eyes of God.   The world
may be on its way toward a better state, if there be anything substantial in our vaunted "progress"; but for the
victims of its evils, here and now, that thought is scarcely
comforting.   By thousands, by millions, they themselves
are being sacrificed for an end—granted the truth of our
social optimism—that they will never see.   By thousands, by millions, they die scarcely knowing why they
struggled and died.   As of the "famous victory," they
inquire with little Peterkin, "What good comes of it at
last?"   Moreover, the goal itself seems uncertain.   All
the progress of the centuries cannot lead to anything
absolutely permanent, in a world destined to ultimate
extinction when the sun's fires cool and the earth becomes, like its attendant moon, an uninhabitable mass
of lifeless matter.   And as for more immediate pros-
pects of social betterment we have, as Mencken says,
"No ground for assuming that the continued progress
visualized by man is in actual accord with the great flow
of elemental forces."   It is at least conceivable that
"devolution is quite as natural as evolution, and may
be just as pleasing, or even a great deal more pleasing,
to God."

It takes high faith to believe that "all shall be well"
in spite of the obvious facts of life which daily experience presents to our view, and particularly those facts
which the study of sociology and economics is laying

bare at the present time—not to mention the war. He must be either extremely callous-hearted or sublimely and blindly optimistic who can realize the cramping, crushing, frustrating effects of much of modern industry and remain unmoved. Only extraordinary conviction can hold that a God of love is truly the Creator of a world in which such conditions exist. Right here, it may be, lies the very greatest difficulty which men experience today in accepting the belief in immortality. How is it possible that man shall survive a world wherein his present condition seems so little the object of divine concern? The universe, apparently, cares next to nothing for man's physical survival; is it then a matter of great consequence whether his soul survive or perish,—his soul, which in the light of naturalism is only the adventitious by-product of certain physical needs and satisfactions? The old doctrine of dualism, and of redemption from a world controlled by evil, and spiritual translation to a world controlled by God, is no longer possible: if the world be rational at all, it is a unity. But both the unity and the rationality of the universe have been renounced in certain contemporary intellectual creeds, for we seem to be at the mercy of blind, irresponsible forces which strike us unawares, whose approach we cannot foresee nor their existence justify. "A microscopic organism invades the human body, and while obeying its own instincts of nutrition and reproduction, blots out a life of inestimable worth to the world." Or war comes, and sweeps the noblest of our youth into the grave. How can a just, not to say loving, God permit this?

The very contemplation of men in the mass supplies difficulties enough, without adding the fact of universal suffering. Is not Lewisohn's conclusion inevitable?— "There is no absolute but life. . . . No God has spoken, no sanction exists." Nevertheless, we continue to live, and are happy; stranger paradox still, we pass on willingly, gladly, the torch of life to others. We refuse to admit the full validity of this suicidal philosophy, and repudiate it in our every act. Whatever disillusionment they have experienced in this life, the majority of human beings are not in the least deterred from handing on the questionable gift to others, who receive it with as blind trust as others have done before them. Nor, like the aged Pheres in Euripides' *Alcestis,* do we cease clinging to life to the very end—even though, in theory, we should scarcely wish to prolong our stay here indefinitely, with our increasing infirmities. Is it because we cannot help ourselves, but succumb to the force which made us and predetermines all our acts, emotions, thoughts? Is it only the biological "will to live" that sustains us? The sense of freedom is too strong in us to admit such a reason today—to excuse ourselves altogether and blame our inconsistency upon the universe.

Instead, we feel that there must be some higher purpose, of which we may not even be conscious, which our individual lives subserve, and by which we in turn as individuals are helped on to greater good.   This deep-seated instinct for life, warped and defiled as it may become, holy and inspiring as it often is; this hunger which no earthly condition, however perfect and harmonious we may imagine it to be, can ever completely satisfy; this instinct to live, this veritably blind "urge" which throbs in the million pulses of humanity, itself leads us to hope for some state of existence where not only the tyrants of earth are cast down from their thrones and mourning ceases and all tears are for ever wiped away, but where men collectively, socially, in eternal fellowship, mingle harmoniously; where each individual's highest end is sought without prejudice to that of any other; and where pain and death and the ancient terror of extinction are forever unknown.   It is more than Utopia that we desire, since even in Utopia men must retain instincts inherited from the brute.   But it is still a society, a fellowship of real persons—not the shadowy wraiths of personified influence, as in George Eliot's "choir invisible."   It can be no blank, empty isolation of the solitary soul if it is truly to satisfy our deepest needs, but must provide for continued companionship, a communion of spirits, an endless converse of mind with kindred mind.   Of this high state the noblest fellowship on earth is only the foretaste and pledge. The association of friends, the companionship of souls knit in bonds of common interest—such as the arts, or letters, or religion, or a common craft, or the mutual love of members of a family—such fellowship encourages us to anticipate one still nobler to be realized hereafter.

> In heaven, perhaps, new chances, one more chance—
> Four great walls in the New Jerusalem,
> Meted on each side by the angel's reed,
> For Leonard, Rafael, Agnolo, and me
> To cover.

III

Can We Still Believe in Immortality?

CAN we still believe in immortality, in view of the findings of modern science and of modern philosophical criticism of those findings? If so, may we still hold to the orthodox Christian conception of the future life? These are our final questions; to answer them has been the purpose of this whole investigation.

It is doubtful if absolute "proofs" of immortality of any sort can be discovered. For modern thought, as for ancient, immortality is still an object of faith. The "evidences" are not complete and final demonstrations, which we may scarcely expect in this present life, but only indications of probability. "Full assurance" lies in another region than that of logical or scientific proof; final conviction involves other factors, moral and spiritual and not purely intellectual, for its support. That is, belief in immortality lies, like all vital beliefs, in a region beyond the range of positive proof and disproof. What modern thought does is shape and express a world-view, more or less unified and more or less commonly accepted, though never final and definitive, in which the age-long, inherited—one might almost say innate or instinctive—belief in immortality either may or may not

120

be maintained. It can neither prove nor disprove immortality; it can only make faith either difficult or easy. As far as modern science and philosophy are concerned, faith in immortality is still no more impossible than it was in the days of Plato or St. Paul or the mediaeval schoolmen; but it is still *faith*. And faith must remain content to exercise its own prerogative, as the self-dedicatory act of our whole being to the best that we know or hope, and not demand proofs in advance, as if we were bargaining with the universe. Nor may we require science to step aside and make room for a conception of "future" life which is only the repetition or prolongation of the present: science will only admit, what indeed the highest religious experience requires, a conception of some other mode of existence, a higher and more transcendent form of self-realization than is possible in this world—the only world with which science has anything to do.

If modern science and philosophy have seemed to destroy or to weaken the empirical evidences for a future life to which our fathers appealed, this may be "not altogether a loss," as Edward Caird once said. Nor need we be unduly concerned if some persons in our time seem little anxious to attain such proofs, final and irrefragable, of the ancient hope. That desire does not necessarily imply a religious temper of mind, or a heart made ready to receive the gift. Indeed, as Caird remarked, "the belief in immortality may easily become an unhealthy preoccupation with a future salvation which prevents us from seeking salvation here," and paralyzes the nerve of social action.   James Ward's comment on this statement is a true one: "This sort of selfish 'otherworldliness' has no doubt called forth condemnation and thus has tended indirectly to discredit the morality of belief in a future life."   Far more grave should be our concern that so many of our fellows lack that spiritual aspiration which alone can lead to the firmest grounds of faith in life eternal, that experience whose ever wider horizons melt at last into the Infinite and the soul discovers its only good in the supreme Goodness upon whom all our hopes at last depend.   "Now I know in part; but then shall I know even as also I have been known."   Yet this is far from the morbid otherworldliness which turned life into a steady contemplation or 'rehearsal' of death, the ultra-ascetic attitude that Plato derived from the *mystae* of his time, and which in a later form obliterated, within three centuries after Christ, the joyous, healthy spirit of the Gospel.   Indeed, the modern world stands closer to St. Paul in spirit. As a whole it echoes Spinoza's saying, "The free man will not spend a long time thinking upon death."   Such an attitude, we believe, is quite consonant with the teaching of our Lord.   "Fear not; it is your Father's good pleasure to give you the Kingdom."   "Take no anxious thought for the morrow"—even the morrow beyond the grave.   In so far as the modern indifference to explicit proofs and the revulsion from a thanato-centric view of life is not indifference to the soul's claim of a higher destiny than that of the body, we may believe that the Christian religion must welcome the freer attitude, the joyous and positive and exuberant confidence which we find widespread today.

Moreover, much of the difficulty which men have experienced in the past, and experience today as well, in accepting the Christian belief, is simply due to our inability to form a coherent notion or concrete picture of an immortal state of being. Our imagination has been nurtured through contact with the world which we see and know—that is, with that fragment of ultimate reality which is expressed here and now in the world that we know and so far as we understand it. Imagination, the only power we possess for clothing that conception with verisimilitude and vividness, is impotent before such a task. Like Columbus and his sailors before they set eyes upon the new world, so for us that life remains an undiscovered country and we cannot hope to describe it. By the same token we must continue to refuse full credence to the Odysseian tales told by other voyagers whose feet have never yet trod the sands of that far shore, and whose stories reflect only too well the familiar, world-old conditions and experiences. Much of the popular conception of the future life is simply "not good enough to be true"; and if literally accepted has the unfortunate result of binding us only the more

firmly to earthly conditions and conceptions.   One may
see a partial explanation of this tendency in the burial
customs of the western world.   How often men think
and speak of the departed as if identified with the physical remains lying in the cemetery or funeral vault!
Christianity repudiates this identification, as the Burial
Office and the Church's customary teaching show.   Yet
the practice of inhumation, and the doctrine of the
resurrection as popularly conceived, present for most
persons insuperable obstacles to a really spiritual conception of the after-life.   It is probable that the Hindu
custom of cremation—which in truth only hastens a
process inevitable in any event—has much to do with
the less materialistic conception of the future life common among India's masses.   We remember the question of Socrates' disciples, "How shall we bury you?"
and his reply: "As you please—only you must catch me
first, and not let me escape you.   I shall not remain
with you after I have drunk the poison, but shall go
away to the happiness of the blest. . . . To use words
wrongly is not only a fault in itself: it also creates evil
in the soul.   You must be of good cheer, and say you
are burying my body; and you must bury it as you
choose."

It is not the hope itself so much as the form in which
it has commonly been conceived and expressed which
science renders untenable.   For that reason alone, it
may be said that few intelligent people look forward

with real satisfaction to the traditional heaven. For heaven, or the after-life, as popularly conceived, is only a glorified reflection of finite and mortal conditions. Must we then admit that "the object of our desire is in fact unknown to us, and unimaginable save in the faintest and most symbolical of adumbrations"—that by heaven we mean "the ultimate term of a process in which we are engaged, of the end of which we can only say that it is good," and nothing more? Yes; and no. For the object of that desire is not altogether "unknown to us." What matters most is the content of that "good" to which we aspire, and for whose realization we unceasingly long. This content, this meaning, the essence of our hope, is at least for Christians a certainty of faith. We "know whom we have believed." It is Christ who illumines that goal of "good": not his words, or his formal teaching, or even his post-resurrection appearances; but Christ himself, a living Person, known through faith, and evermore known more fully and deeply as Christian experience advances. Like the dying thief to whom he promised, "Today shalt thou be with me in Paradise," and the man died content in company with his new-found Lord, so the Christian disciple looks forward to meeting Christ, to a joyful reunion and recognition—under whatever conditions that meeting may take place after death. And to be with Christ "is Paradise enow." Like the pagan poet who would fain have died were he only sure to meet Euripides in the great Beyond, so the Christian willingly faces death in the assurance that "to depart and be with Christ . . . is far better." It is "because he lives" that we shall live also. It is not by any mere word here and there that we prove our resurrection by the resurrection of Christ: it is the sum of our knowledge of him. As Bishop Charles Slattery said, "He who identified himself with men's weakness will identify men with his strength."

In fine, it is a spiritual experience, not a process of logical proof, that underlies the Christian belief in immortality. For this reason the historical, critical evaluation of the resurrection narratives in the New Testament does not vitally affect Christian belief in immortality. Faith does not stand or fall with the historicity of these or any other similar accounts. Upon purely historical grounds, the Christian scholar may defend—and with good hope of success—the historical truth of those appearances. Without them, the earliest history of the Christian movement is unexplained. How did the worship of Christ ever arise in first-century Palestine and spread generally throughout the Roman Empire, if the experiences described in the Church's earliest documents never took place? Nor do these narratives read like the fictions of imaginative minds or the off-spring of credulous fancy. It is the unanimous view of the New Testament writers, and the testimony of their sources, that Jesus arose from the grave *as Messiah*.

"Thus it behoved the Christ to suffer these things and to enter into his glory." The resurrection of Jesus alone did not produce the faith in his Messiahship, for without such antecedent belief the resurrection appearances might never have been interpreted Messianically, that is, as proofs of his continued and now fully-realized Messiahship. Nor were the appearances understood simply as proofs of Jesus' survival and entrance upon immortality—since that belief was already held, without such proofs. It was as a divine being, the Son of God, that Jesus rose from the dead, not just one immortal soul among many. The Christian belief in immortality is not based, and never has been based, either in the New Testament or in later Christianity, upon the historical fact of Jesus' resurrection. The faith of the earliest Christians was not so founded, since their belief in a future life was antecedent to their belief in Jesus' Messiahship. Nor has historical Christianity so interpreted the resurrection; it was not in proof that we and all other human beings shall survive death that our Lord rose from the grave. The Christian belief is that "in Christ," victorious over death, and through "the power of his resurrection," through union and communion with our risen, ascended Lord, "we too shall live." It was not in the course of some kind of ancient psychical research that Christians seized upon the fact of Jesus' triumph over death; rather, here was the open gateway by which men might, in and through the power of Christ who is "the Way and the Truth," "the Resurrection and the Life," themselves enter into eternal happiness. As the Christian hope rests upon grounds outside the range of science, so likewise are its ultimate evidences independent of an interpretation of historical documents and data. Though we are by no means prepared to abandon the history, we may nevertheless affirm that no criticism, no neutralizing of the historical testimony, no reinterpretation of the facts can touch the secret source of Christian conviction. That rests secure in a personal spiritual experience of newness of life through Christ.

§

If we go back now and consider the specific conceptions of the after-life which traditional orthodox Christianity has maintained, it may be that in the light of modern knowledge certain modifications in their formal expression are required.

First of all, the belief that this present life is one of "probation," and that there is no further probation after death, would seem to be supported by modern ethical and philosophical thought. If the future life be another mode of existence, whose conditions we cannot define; if, as seems likely, the time-process of the physical universe has no part in those conditions; if the soul or "self" is born in this world as the fruit of biological and psychological processes, and begins a real and determinative experience here; if the after-life is the projection—"the wages of going on"—and the fuller realization of this self; then it would seem inexcusable, upon the basis of our science and philosophy, as well as of Christian faith, to "neglect so great a salvation" as is offered us here, in the self-indulgent confidence of making good present losses hereafter.

> Will they
> Who failed under the heat of this life's day
> Support the fervors of the heavenly morn?
> No, no! the energy of life may be
> Kept on after the grave, but not begun;
> And he who flagged not in the earthly strife,
> From strength to strength advancing,—only he,
> His soul well-knit, and all his battles won,
> Mounts, and that hardly, to eternal life.

We must not of course presume to dogmatize, and deny the hope that there are "in heaven, perhaps, new chances, one more chance"; Christian theology does not so dogmatize but concedes that in the mercy of God there may possibly be other opportunities for repentance, for restoration, for the awakening unto life. Not only is this prospect held out for the heathen who have not heard the message of salvation or who died before the coming of Christ, but even for those Christians who die unrepentant, as in the quaint intercession of the Prayer Book: "If it be thy will, preserve his life, that there may be place for repentance; but if thou hast otherwise appointed, let thy mercy supply to him the want of the usual opportunity for the trimming of his lamp." Nor must we presume to pass judgment upon the success or failure of other lives. As the angelic chorus sings at the end of *Faust*,

> Wer immer strebend sich bemüht,
> Den können wir erlösen

—"he who with ceaseless effort strives, we can set free." But theology and ethics alike insist that "now it is high time to awake out of sleep; the night is far spent, the day is at hand." Of any further probation beyond this life we have not the slightest evidence. Whatever we may hope for others, no one may presume upon further probation for himself! And to this earnest exhortation modern science and philosophy sternly add: We know nothing of a soul distinct from the habits and laws of the individual life; the only "self" is that which emerges here in the course of personal experience; how then can we begin to "grow a self" when these conditions have, for all that we know, come to an end? How can that possibly survive which has never begun to exist? As well wish to preserve the apples from a tree that never bore fruit! Thus science deepens our sense of the tremendous issues of the present life, and by no means warrants a procrastinating lethargy and indifference. If this life means anything at all, we must bend every effort towards the fullest possible realization of that meaning here and now. So and so only can we think of its continuance, and the continuance of its meaning, in a life beyond.

But what of the old, literal, cosmological ideas of heaven and hell that inspired the minds of our fore-fathers with fervent zeal and awe? Under the influence of such conceptions they were ready to "work out their own salvation, with fear and trembling." In place of these ideas we sometimes meet today with the easy assumption that somewhere, somehow, under some condition or other, "all men live for ever." There is no compelling power in such a belief. It is neither a real faith nor even a positive hope. It inspires no ardor of desire, no zeal of effort, no sense of the issues involved in mere living. It has value neither for moral growth nor for the biological life-process. At best it is only a barren optimism, without philosophical or religious significance, and the future which it assumes is void of meaning. To this assumption, it is certain, science lends no support; and there is no certainty that the optimism is well founded. We may still be required to "win" salvation, "gain" eternal life, or receive it as the gift of God. A true *faith* in immortality, if not immortality itself, appears always to be morally conditioned. "The right to speak about the eternal values," as Inge says, "the right even to believe in them, must be earned by strict self-discipline." "Some touch of heroic self-abnegation is necessary before we can have a soul which death cannot touch." There must be, for each one of us, something which makes our immortality eternally worth while, if we are to share the high faith of those who ventured their all for God "in the confidence of a certain faith, in the comfort of a reasonable, religious, and holy hope." Only the man who believes his life supremely worth living can venture to assume his own immortality beyond death.

§

What shall we say of the Church's ancient doctrine of the Intermediate State, and of its corollaries—such as the invocation of saints, intercessions for the departed, the belief in their prayers for us? There can be no doubt that the too-explicit, geographical conception of the after-life which appealed to "the ages of faith" is not relished by modern minds. At least, we say, it belongs to the poetry of religion, to the realm of fancy and symbol—a realm where the final authority is taste, and where taste has the right to change. Yet some attitude or other we must take; for such fancies—supposing them nothing more—determine the daily practice of religion. And just as we found that ethical considerations support the Christian idea of probation, so the feelings and affections, the ethical outlook, the sense of duty and obligation to those we love, require us to trust where we may not see, and pray where we are not forbidden. If the immortal life be the uninterrupted continuation of the quest for God and for His goodness; if spiritual progress is real "there" as "here"; then we may continue to conceive the life to come under some such form as that in which traditional Christianity has represented it. "The wages of going on, and not to fail," assuredly implies "other tasks in other lives, God willing," as new stages are reached in the soul's advance. And we can conceive no limit short of God Himself, the attainment of perfection in union with the Eternal. With Ulysses and his fellow-voyagers, we may say that our

> purpose holds
> To sail beyond the sunset, and the baths
> Of all the western stars.

Nothing short of final union with God, no incidental "rewards," no preparative and intermediate satisfactions of the soul, can end the divine restlessness which the Creator planted in us when He "made us for Himself." Our journey is "unto the Infinite."

> And though thy soul sail leagues and leagues beyond—
> Still, leagues beyond those leagues, there is more sea.

The journey is unending, for the goal ever recedes as we approach it; but our joy increases with each advancing stage—there is no weariness or exhaustion, or disappointment, but ever deepening satisfaction.

"Great is your reward in heaven," said our Lord. But he never defined what that meant. It is likely, however, that he implied more and not less than even the holiest of his disciples have supposed. And must we not assume that those who have already "entered into the joy of their Lord" are blessed with a happiness beyond all earthly joys—in the enjoyment of knowledge, of insight, of strength, of holiness, of love?   The words of Dean Church are full of appeal to modern men and women: "Their joy is in complete liberation of the spirit—strength of heart for all service, vigor of mind for all truth, purity of nature for the vision of God.   It will mean for the soul, not the backward but the forward look, not skirting the shore in gladness that the perils of the voyage are over, but spreading the sail with confident hope, and seeking port after port in the sublime adventure of knowing God."   The secret of that progressive transformation, so the Christian religion teaches, is the union of the soul with God, its Source of life; and the divine likeness into which it grows, "from glory to glory," is "the face of God unveiled in Christ Jesus."   This union, and the resulting transformation, begin in time.   "For this purpose was the Son of God manifested," that he might make us even now the children of God and heirs of eternal life. This union and transformation, according to Christian theology, are really implicit in the creation of man's soul "in the image and likeness of God."   But their realization is beyond time and place; it is in the Infinite. All that Christ was and is, all that he is as perfect Man and true God, we must share, and in a sense become, in him.

Viewed then in the light of this high Christian conception of the life to come, what shall we say of prayers for the departed?   Must our Protestant neglect of such devotions continue, as if our loved ones had somehow no further need of our prayers, or could receive no benefit from them?   It would seem that modern thought, on the contrary, demands that if prayer be real or effective at all it shall not cease when those who have gone before advance, as by a bend in the road, beyond our sight. The experience of many devout souls in time of war, when prayers unnumbered are offered to God for men at the front—who may be meeting death long before the news reaches us—this experience naturally raises the question, When must we cease to pray for them?   And the answer which comes intuitively to thousands of praying hearts is this: Cease not to pray!   For they are living still, in this world or the other, and still have need of prayers!   Somewhere in God's great universe they are; in some state of life, this or another, they still live. Out of sight in Europe or beyond the Pacific, thousands of miles away, or out of sight on the other side of death, they live and pray, and we too may pray for them! This profoundly real experience and conviction we Protestants ought frankly to recognize in our public worship.   Upon Christian principles, the demand for the right to pray for the dead is both reasonable and reverent.   It springs from a deeper faith, and from no revival of pagan superstition, or merely from "Catholic influence in the army." For the faith out of which it springs is far more essentially and natively Christian than the quasi-fatalistic theology of the sixteenth century, which has effectively forbidden the use of such prayers among us for too many generations. May it not be that one factor in the decline of faith in immortality at the present day is this very refusal of many Christians to follow the dictates of the believing heart and pray for those who have gone before?—and to ask, if it be God's will, that we may likewise receive the benefit of their prayers for us?

But grant this, it will be urged, and the invocation of saints will follow; the door will be open for all manner of pre-Reformation abuses to creep in! To which we may reply, The only test is reality; if the departed live and are conscious and continue their life of prayer, raised now to a higher level of more immediate converse with God, then those who have been the subjects of their prayer in this world may well remain—and may request to remain—the subjects of their prayer still. There may, indeed, for all we know to the contrary, take place some sort of intuitive realization that this is so in fact, as when the Bishops at Chalcedon cried, "The martyr Flavian is praying for us"; though we should naturally expect such intuitions to come rather in the quiet of private devotion or in the sacred hour of communion.

'Tis here I feel how near thou art,
Thy face I almost see,
When in the Eucharist I touch
   The hand that touches thee.

Of course, a mechanical and artificial theory of the merits of such prayer, or a presumptuous reliance upon its efficacy, not to say the bold intrusion of our petty requests upon the attention of a beatified soul in the Beyond, leads both belief and practice outside the realm of vital religious experience.

§

The traditional formulation of the doctrines of heaven and hell, as places or states of the finally good and bad, bears plainly enough the marks of its origin in primitive thought, inherited by Christianity from the Jewish apocalyptic writings of the period in which our religion arose. Reflecting the modern reaction to this formulation, Lowes Dickinson held that most men would prefer extinction to an immortality involving both heaven and hell—even interpreting heaven to mean "all that the noblest men would desire," and hell "all that the basest men would fear." Hell he regarded "with something approaching horror." "As to the improvement of the criminal, that is ruled out in the Christian hell, for it is precisely part of his punishment that he is, and knows himself to be, eternally wicked."

But as we have already suggested, the psychological

foundations of these and other Christian doctrines lie deep in the experience of the race. The doctrine of eternal punishment is a case in point. The idea of hell may have originated, in part, in such mental states as that of the Psalmist who wrote, "Thy terrors have I suffered with a troubled mind." The sense of God's wrath has played a widespread and important part in the history of religious thought, almost up to the present day. But it seems more likely, as we study its beginnings in religious literature, that the conception originated in the experience of persecution or oppression and in the emotions which that experience aroused. It was so in Jewish and early Christian apocalyptic and in Greek mythology; the deaths of the persecutors and their punishment after death must befit and be commensurate with their tyrannies and oppressions while they lived. Otherwise they will get off far too easily! This is the sense of the imprecatory Psalms, and they should so be read—if read at all: "Let *him* be cast down," as he cast down others; "let *his* children beg their bread," since it was he who impoverished others, and their famished children sickened and died; let *Babylon's* infants perish, as our babes perished at Babylon's ruthless hands! It is not the noblest of motives that we discover here, but at least one somewhat less inhuman than pure malice and vindictiveness. Of course, the anticipated earthly punishments frequently failed to take place; and so, with the rise of individualism and of belief in immortality, resurrection, and future judgment, they were postponed to the after-life, and the pious if vengeful imagination of the victims elaborated and refined the torments that oppressors and persecutors were expected to suffer in the world to come. In the end, it may really be doubted if any human being was ever so wicked as to deserve for ever the full torments of Tartarus and Gehenna, of Virgil's Hades, or the Inferno of Dante and Milton. As Plotinus held, "Vice even at its worst is still human, still carries some trace of good." Added to this, the modern psychological study of crime tends to mitigate the responsibility of the individual and to shift a considerable share of it upon environment and heredity, in a word, upon society itself. So too the latest psychoanalysis finds motives of good as well as of evil lying deep within the unconscious mind. Man may lose "the likeness of God," theology holds, but "the image of God" he retains for ever and ever. And if that image be indelibly engraved upon his very nature, so that he can cease to be like God in some respect only by ceasing to be human, then there must remain hope for the ultimate restoration—somehow, beyond all that we can imagine—even of those who seem to us irrevocably hardened in sin.

To the modern mind, normally humanitarian in its sentiments, this hope is not only appealing but inevitable. In a universe which is finally to be entirely subject to its Creator, "that God may be all in all," there is ultimately no room for an eternal hell, not even for one most subtly refined and spiritual; no, nor even for the concept of such a state as "everlasting damnation."   We are dealing, of course, with a state of mind or, rather, a state of will—not with a place.   But there need be no fear that, once the terrors of a material hell are banished from men's thoughts, they will cease to fear punishment and plunge into the depths of sin and vice.   The hell that we make for ourselves through remorse of conscience, the "sense of loss" and the realization that we have outraged the highest Love, this hell is terrible enough; and as long as an ethical experience remains possible for man, and we continue to do what we would not and to will what we do not, this hell will remain. Yet even these torments, far more painful than any "pain of sense," are remedial and disciplinary.   "The wages of sin is death": this meant to St. Paul the physical doom of death that has overtaken the race descended from Adam, in that every man has shared Adam's sinful nature.   But taking the word as popularly understood, "death," even the "second death," is scarcely a fit name for a state in which no amount of torture can produce insensibility, and in which animation continues for ever for the very purpose of prolonging pain.   Nor is it the just penalty for sin that one should be engulfed eternally in ever deeper depths of wickedness, punishment only adding to the will's obduracy, until the soul is finally swallowed up in loathsomeness, the sin it loves and itself become inseparably one and meriting as one the endless wrath of God. No man is bad enough to merit, nor is God the "man of wrath" required to inflict, such a stupid, meaningless, and abhorrent penalty. Not so are the ways of Infinite Wisdom and Love. The mad dream but reflects all too clearly the crude and stupid criminology of long ago.

The real hell which we suffer, and may suffer hereafter, the real heaven we enjoy, here and hereafter, is within ourselves.

I myself am heaven and hell.

The degree of spiritual and moral attainment of any person may be measured by the intensity of his realization of the meaning of these spiritual states. They are, as the author of *Theologia Germanica* says, "two good, safe ways for man to travel in this present time." They reflect, positively and negatively, the meaning to the human soul of a clear conscience and a conscious communion with God. And if modern reaction from the crude, materialistic notions of an earlier age has resulted, for the present, in a somewhat nonchalant indifference to the moral issues which underlay originally, and have supported historically, the traditional conceptions, we can only say that time will surely bring a change. It would certainly be pessimism to assume that men generally will respond only to a warning of future punishment, and remain indifferent to the spiritual tidings of eternal life!   Some better, truer, fairer symbol of Eternal Justice will take the place of these conceptions, and men who no longer have any fear of hell will still respect the unchanging law of right and wrong: "Whatsoever a man soweth, that shall he also reap." Biology, perhaps, or medicine, or chemistry, may supply that symbol—not criminal law; for law is always relatively antiquated, whereas science is progressive. And it is science, not legislation, which in this age gives us our profoundest clues to reality, and provides the metaphors and symbols in which our deepest thought is expressed.

§

If we thus give up the traditional conception of heaven and hell, and substitute some more satisfactory symbol of the spiritual and psychological truth for which it stands, how fare the remaining factors in orthodox Christian eschatology—the resurrection and final judgment, the whole program of the "last things" derived by early Christianity from contemporary Judaism? As for the resurrection of the *body*—a conception, as we have seen, not to be identified with the resurrection of the flesh—this seems still to imply, for all its improvement upon the cruder doctrine, a survival in space and time.   Indeed, the risen body remains in the same old world we have known all along, only glorified and

transformed.   But if heaven—or hell—be not a place,
what further need have we for bodies?   It is a speculation for which we have no data, scientific or other.   The
relations of body and mind in the present life are not
as yet satisfactorily defined; neither is the conception
of "matter" and its possible transformations.   If Bergson is right in supposing that mind and matter, soul and
body, are essentially or originally of the same stuff,
energy, *élan vital;* if monism is correct in its fundamental hypothesis; then the persistence beyond death of
the self or soul, as the highest personal energy, implies
necessarily the survival of the "body"—a body of some
kind—as the point or focus of this highest energy in its
impact upon lower and degraded forms of energy, "the
spent rockets falling earthward."   At the least, we may
say that the mystery of the soul is not greater than the
mystery of energy and matter.   Why matter should
exist, what it is, and why there exists a material universe
at all, are insoluble questions up to the present.

As the physical resurrection, popularly conceived, is
almost meaningless for the modern conception of immortality, so the Last Judgment fits ill with the modern
view of time and universal progress.   For the first conception, however, an equivalent is found in the assurance of personal identity and survival apart from the
body of flesh—an identity which is nowise dependent
upon a certain collocation of chemical elements, since
what we essentially are is spirit, not flesh.   So likewise,

perhaps, an equivalent for the belief in the Last Judgment may be found in the assurance that there is one absolute law by which all men are finally—and always—to be judged; that this is not a morally relative or indifferent universe, but through all the tangled skein of circumstance and change runs a subtle moral and spiritual law whose existence man ignores at his peril, a law as inescapable as the laws of chemistry or biology; that none can escape this law, and that ultimately every soul must be measured by an absolute standard; that God has a plan and purpose for every individual life; and that the standard of human excellence is Christ. The earliest Christians of course already believed in a final judgment, before they became followers of Christ; what they added to this belief was the identification of the Messianic Judge with Jesus Christ.   It is the loving, merciful Christ who is nevertheless the wholly just Arbiter of men's destinies.   The judgment will therefore be perfectly just, for the Supreme Love never errs.   He will account sins of omission on the part of the righteous as equally grave with sins of commission on the part of the wicked.   The thoughts of men's hearts will be revealed; secret acts of generosity or of unselfish service will stand clear in his sight.   His sentence will be, "Inasmuch as ye did it—or did it not—unto one of the least of these my brethren, ye did it—or did it not—unto me."

It is the ethical value which is uppermost in this doctrine of the judgment, just as in the doctrine of resurrection it is the guarantee of personal identity which is the primary concern. Though we may recognize as symbolic every one of the details of the judgment as pictured in Christian apocalypse or hymn, the principle underlying the whole conception admits no explaining-away. It is simple truth, that somewhere there runs an undeviating line of division between right and wrong; and that sin, the conscious love of wrong-doing, is for ever displeasing to God, while goodness, virtue, self-discipline are for ever pleasing to Him. These truths, however, would seem to be safeguarded sufficiently by the belief in an immediate judgment, which is to take place after death and before the final judgment. It is a belief which theology has recognized; and though itself "symbolic" it is almost the only available symbol in which to set forth what seems most probable in itself—the soul's awaking to a recognition of the divine justice, the first clear view of things in the light of new and endless day, the deepening distaste for all evil and the widening love for all good. The "judgment" must be spiritual, in the deepest sense; it must take place in us. And here also science may some day provide us a fairer, truer symbol than that of the court-room and the prison-house.

§

If the life begun here and continued hereafter is one of endless progress, it is obvious that the "end" of our

course can be designated only in the faintest symbols.
No categorical description can adequately represent it.
The negative language of the mystics may impress us as
barren and unsatisfying, as when they speak of a state
"beyond being" or of "no-being"; but we must remember that they are endeavoring to state in intelligible
words what really transcends definition; it is like the
mathematical symbol of infinity. The marked reticence of our Lord, with his emphasis upon values which
we can understand here and now in the light of present
experience, is wiser than the doctrines of the seers.   By
faith

> Our souls have sight of that immortal sea
> Which brought us hither;

but we have not as yet, and may never have, a vision of
its farther shores, if that sea be in fact "the shoreless,
boundless ocean."   Intuitive knowledge may give us
some foretaste of what that life beyond is like, as in
St. Augustine's "moment of intelligence"; but it is
something qualitative, not quantitative, and it still
lies beyond definition.   Though real, the goal is reces-
sive.   We find even here in this life many things that
are really good; "but there are always other and better
beyond."   Hence "it is hazardous to fix one's ideal and
say, finally, This or that would be heaven.   For we may
find, as did the voyagers in Browning's *Paracelsus,* that
the real heaven lies always beyond."   By pureness, by
knowledge, by the realization of unselfish love for oth-

ers, by fellowship in all that is truest and best in our life, men may rise to heights of vision and possess a certainty of faith which no longer seeks to behold "the end from the beginning." It is enough to believe that hereafter "we shall know even as we are known," even though for the present we see "as in a glass darkly." Yet if the best that we know on earth be permanently good, to be known as good hereafter, we may be sure that individual personality must remain to the end, identified as it is with that good, in love with it, and ever enriched and strengthened through still further realization of the divine goodness and love—

> The Love that moves the sun in heaven
> And all the stars.

And as we grow in love we shall find more objects of our love; we shall discover hidden and hitherto unsuspected works of the divine goodness, much as we find ever new attractions in noble works of human art, and, supremely, in the souls of those persons whom we love. And as love is the guiding power behind the universe, so is it likewise "the hierophant of all the divine mysteries." "In thy light shall we see light." This personality of which we speak, whose final fruition is an endless life in God, is certainly more than the finite ego—which, even upon our present plane of experience, is scarcely a man's real self. There is a field of personal life above consciousness, just as there is one below it.

What we love in a friend is not the finite individual, but "the Christ in him"; not what he is now so much as what he is becoming.   The truth of this is even clearer when we consider a parent's love for his child.   And with the final liberation of this personality, after the breaking down of successive barriers to its full development and expression, there must be not only a greater expansion and intensification of its life—new powers, new vision, new realization—but also, in fellowship with others, a greater love.   It is not "impersonal immortality" that Christianity promises us, nor that modern men and women long to attain; it is a personal life fully realized beyond and outside all finite conditions and limitations, at unity with itself and with all others, at peace in God.

This principle taken alone, without any attempt to formulate in earthly terms the ineffable and transcendent which lies beyond, is sufficient to enable us to believe in immortality in the light of modern knowledge, and in immortality essentially as Christianity has always conceived and represented it.   No earlier age has placed such value upon human personality as does our own. For all the horrors perpetrated upon earth in this generation it is still true that our literature, our political doctrines, our religious beliefs find the meaning of life summed up in that one word.   And personality as we know it is a growing thing, for whose development apparently no limits can be set.   And its greatest means of growth is through the realization of unselfish love. "Behold, now are we the sons of God, and it doth not yet appear what we shall be; but we know that, when he shall appear, we shall be like him; for we shall see him as he is. And everyone that hath this hope in him purifieth himself, even as he is pure." Finally it is the Gospel of Christ that has given us our highest conception of the capacities of personality, as it has supplied our noblest ideas of human destiny. It is to this Gospel that men still turn for assurance of the reality and for the justification of their dearest hopes. And they do not turn in vain.

A Selected Bibliography

BAILLIE, JOHN. *And the Life Everlasting* (Scribner).

BEVAN, EDWYN R. *The Hope of a World to Come* (Allen and Unwin).

BRIGHTMAN, E. S. *Immortality in Post-Kantian Idealism* (Harvard).

BROWN, W. ADAMS. *The Christian Hope* (Scribner).

CHARLES, R. H. *Eschatology: Hebrew, Jewish, and Christian* (Black).

CUMONT, F. *After Life in Roman Paganism* (Yale).

DENNEY, J. *Factors of Faith in Immortality* (Hodder and Stoughton).

DICKINSON, G. LOWES. *Religion and Immortality* (Dent).

FALCONER, R. A. *The Idea of Immortality and Western Civilization* (Harvard).

FARNELL, L. R. *Greek Hero Cults and Ideas of Immortality* (Oxford).

FENN, W. W. *Immortality and Theism* (Harvard).

FISKE, JOHN. *The Destiny of Man Viewed in the Light of His Origin* (Houghton, Mifflin).

FISKE, JOHN. *Life Everlasting* (Houghton, Mifflin).

FOSDICK, H. E. *The Assurance of Immortality* (Macmillan).

FOSDICK, H. E. *Spiritual Values and Eternal Life* (Harvard).

GALLOWAY, GEORGE. *The Idea of Immortality, Its Development and Value* (Clark).

GATES, A. A. *My Belief in Immortality: A Symposium* (Doubleday, Doran).

GAYFORD, S. C. *The Future State* (Rivingtons).

GORDON, GEORGE A. *Immortality and the New Theodicy* (Houghton, Mifflin).

GRIFFIN, N. E. *The Farther Shore* (Houghton, Mifflin).

GRIFFITH-JONES, E. *Faith and Immortality: A Study of the Christian Doctrine of the Life to Come* (Duckworth).

HAYNES, E. S. P. *The Belief in Personal Immortality* (Putnam).

INGE, W. R. "Survival and Immortality," in *Outspoken Essays*, vol. ii (Longmans).

JAMES, W. *Human Immortality: Two Supposed Objections to the Doctrine* (Houghton, Mifflin).

JAMES, W. "Personal Immortality," in *Essays*.

JONES, W. TUDOR. *Metaphysics of Life and Death* (Doran).

LAKE, K. *Immortality and the Modern Mind* (Harvard).

Lodge, O. J. *Science and Immortality* (Moffat, Yard).

Lyman, E. W. *The Meaning of Selfhood and Faith in Immortality* (Harvard).

Mackenzie, W. D. *Man's Consciousness of Immortality* (Harvard).

Marchant, James (ed.). *Immortality* (Putnam).

Matthews, W. R. (ed.). *King's College Lectures on Immortality* (Univ. of London Press).

McComb, S. *The Future Life in the Light of Modern Inquiry* (Dodd, Mead).

McTaggart, J. Ellis. *Human Immortality and Pre-Existence* (Arnold).

Mellone, S. H. "Immortality," in the *Encyclopaedia of Religion and Ethics*, vol. vii (Scribner).

Moore, C. H. *Ancient Beliefs in the Immortality of the Soul* (Longmans).

Moore, C. H. *The Religious Thought of the Greeks* (Harvard).

Moore, G. F. *Metempsychosis* (Harvard).

Münsterberg, H. *The Eternal Life* (Houghton, Mifflin).

Myers, F. W. H. *Science and a Future Life* (Macmillan).

Osler, W. *Science and Immortality* (Houghton, Mifflin).

Palmer, F. *The Winning of Immortality* (Crowell).

Palmer, G. H. *Intimations of Immortality in the Sonnets of Shakspere* (Houghton, Mifflin).

Pringle-Pattison, A. S. *The Idea of Immortality* (Oxford).

Ryle, H. E. *Life after Death* (Scott).

Salmond, S. D. F. *The Christian Doctrine of Immortality* (Clark).

Slattery, C. L. *The Gift of Immortality* (Houghton, Mifflin).

Slattery, C. L. *Life Beyond Life* (Longmans).

Smyth, J. P. *The Gospel of the Hereafter* (Revell).

Smyth, Newman. *Modern Belief in Immortality* (Scribner).

Simpson, J. Y. *Man and the Attainment of Immortality* (Hodder and Stoughton).

Snowden, J. H. *The Christian Belief in Immortality in the Light of Modern Thought* (Macmillan).

Streeter, B. H. (ed.). *Immortality* (Macmillan).

Storr, V. F. *Christianity and Immortality* (Longmans).

Temple, Wm. *The Idea of Immortality in Relation to Religion and Ethics* (Independent Press).

Von Hügel, F. *Eternal Life* (Clark).

Whitehead, A. N. *Religion in the Making* (Macmillan).

Whitehead, A. N. *Science and the Modern World* (Macmillan).

DATE DUE

NOV 10 '76			
NOV 1 1 1977			
FEB 1 8 1981			
DEC 0 5 1984			
DEC 1 6 1987			
OCT 1 7 1990			
DEC 1 2 1990			

DEMCO 38-297